Mark,
God Bless you!.
John as

John Morgan is a wonderful and uniquely talented individual. I have enjoyed his wit, charm, and above all, his honest passion for the Lord. My favorite book, other than the Bible, is Thomas à Kempis's *The Imitation of Christ*, and I have always enjoyed talking with John about the amazing opportunity we have as Christians to imitate our Savior. I believe you'll enjoy him, too.

—TODD AGNEW
SINGER/SONGWRITER OF THE
WORSHIP SONG "GRACE LIKE RAIN"

John Morgan joined us onstage before 300,000 people on NewSong's 2007 Winter Jam Tour Spectacular. Every night, we marveled that the Lord not only gave John the "amazing face" of President George W. Bush but also the "amazing grace" to use his comedic impersonation as a platform to encourage all of us to imitate Christ.

—EDDIE CARSWELL
FOUNDING MEMBER OF THE
GRAMMY-NOMINATED GROUP NEWSONG
CO-PRODUCER OF WINTER JAM

How does a man with a talent for imitating others find his own true voice? John Morgan's spiritual journey is an engaging and inspiring story, told with refreshing candor by a genuine Christian who also happens to be a first-rate entertainer. I was hooked from the first page.

—NATE LARKIN
CONFERENCE SPEAKER AND
AUTHOR OF *SAMSON AND THE PIRATE MONKS*

I know John to be passionate, warm, and incredibly funny. His story challenges, blesses, and is filled with God's transforming power.

—DONNA VANLIERE
NEW YORK TIMES BESTSELLING AUTHOR OF
THE CHRISTMAS HOPE SERIES AND
THE ANGELS OF MORGAN HILL

It's joy as a pastor and worship leader to have a man who is committed to the local church. Above his own success John has led his family to see Metro Life Church as the dearest place on Earth. And for that, I could not be more grateful.

—TODD TWINING
PASTOR AND WORSHIP LEADER
METRO LIFE CHURCH
ORLANDO, FLORIDA

My Life
as a
Bush
... and my heart for
imitating Jesus

My Life
as a
Bush
... and my heart for
imitating Jesus

JOHN MORGAN
with Vince Wilcox

CREATION
HOUSE
A STRANG COMPANY

My Life as a Bush by John Morgan with Vince Wilcox
Published by Creation House
A Strang Company
600 Rinehart Road
Lake Mary, Florida 32746
www.creationhouse.com

Design Director: Bill Johnson

Cover design by Karen Grindley

Cover photo by Jon Morgan, jonmorganphotography.com

Copyright © 2008 by John Morgan
All rights reserved

Library of Congress Control Number: 2008929918
International Standard Book Number: 978-1-59979-459-4

First Edition

08 09 10 11 12 — 9 8 7 6 5 4 3 2 1
Printed in the United States of America

This book is affectionately dedicated
to my wife, Kathy,
and to our sons,
Christopher, Stephen, Daniel, and Jonathan,
and loving daughter-in-law, Emily.
I love you so much.

ACKNOWLEDGMENTS

First and foremost, thanks to God, who created and redeemed me to be like His Son, Jesus.

Unimaginable gratitude and heartfelt love to:

- My precious wife and best friend, Kathy; and my children, Christopher (an example of servanthood and love), Stephen (my adventurer and videographer), Daniel (my encourager and vocal coach), and Jonathan (the source of so much joy)

- Mom and Dad, Chuck and Eileen Morgan. You are my inspiration.

- My immediate and extended family, especially my sisters, Janice, who dove into the trenches for me time and time again; Mary Ann, whose unconditional love has been the source of so much encouragement; and Becky, my "hearing from God" partner

- My mom-in-law, Julie, whose love and support helped carry us through the lean years

- My third mom, Averill—my gratitude for you is eternal. I still run to you for prayer.

- My sister-in-law, Susan, whose help and support was my catalyst for success

- Our pastor, Danny Jones, whom God used to thresh away so much chaff

- Mike Gilland, Joel Balin, Paul Balluff, Brian Wells, Bob Anderson, Rob Oleck, Patsy Gilbert, and Patsy Luther whose influence and friendship have truly shaped my life
- Todd Twining, who has led our church family through the gates of splendor into God's presence every Sunday for many years
- Duane Ward and the whole team at Premiere Speakers, for representing me to the world
- The event planners, talent agencies, TV producers, and other individuals who gave me a shot
- Lynn McCain and McCain & Co. Public Relations, for getting the word out so well
- Jon Morgan, for taking "the money shot"
- Gloria Green, who put the bat in my hands
- Pamela Muse, Ben Greene, Tom Jackson, and World Vision, for allowing me to be part of changing a child's life
- Promise Keepers, for letting the truth be told
- Ryan Stout and SLD Interactive, for online services
- Thoughts.com, for being a great place to post my written and video blogs
- NewSong, WinterJam, The Premier Group, Troy VanLiere, and Sarah Drumheller, for putting me in the bus, in the plane, and on the boat
- Lisa Saffron, the "Cruise Doctor"

- Tom Walter, Bill Gray, Tim Gray, and all the folks around the world who have served in the faux Secret Service
- Michael Nolan, for putting really funny words in my mouth
- Teresa Barnwell, for being the best Hillary ever
- Justin Finnell, who taught me how to be funny
- Paula Olson, who kept insisting that I give this a try
- Bea Fogelman and Gregg Thompson, who helped me get started in this amazing industry
- the family of professional look-alikes who welcomed me in
- RW Phipps & Company, for keeping the books
- Steve Blount, for the treasure of your insight and assistance
- Stephen Strang and Strang Communications (especially Allen Quain, Ginny Maxwell, Atalie Anderson, Amanda Lowell, and Robert Caggiano, among countless others) whose vision, faith, and miraculous turnaround time helped make this book a reality
- my manager, great friend, and co-writer, Vince Wilcox, for your honesty, integrity, and brotherhood
- Gov. Mike Huckabee, for writing the foreword of this book and for being an extraordinary public servant
- President George W. Bush—Sir, it is an honor to be your look-alike!

CONTENTS

FOREWORD

JOHN MORGAN HAS entertained millions of people with his impersonations of George W. Bush as the president of the United States. Not only does he look and sound like George W. Bush, he even seems to act like the president.

It may seem easy to pretend to be someone else, especially if you resemble that person, but John shows us how he had to "learn" to be George W. Bush. More importantly, he takes us on an intimate, personal journey illustrating how and why we all should become impersonators of the Greatest Person who ever lived.

While he has made America laugh, John now makes us think about whom we all should be trying to impersonate. Through his experiences in pretending to be the president, John grew to better understand what it means to "impersonate" Christ, and why our ultimate goal in life should be to be more like Christ. We all can apply the lessons John learned from impersonating the president to imitating Jesus Christ in our lives, starting with reading and understanding His words.

With encouraging stories and humorous anecdotes, John Morgan conveys a significant and serious message, a message of the ultimate impersonation. While we often have been instructed to model our lives after Christ, John uses humor and his keen insights to tell us in another way we should imitate Christ in our lives.

You are about to read a book that will take you on a remarkable journey as John asks you questions at the end of every chapter requiring reflection, reaction, and ultimately, personal action.

It is my sincere hope that you will take the time to read this book and to ask your own questions and see what kind of answers you get and actions you take.

It is a funny book, but do not "misunderestimate" the power of this book.

—Governor Mike Huckabee

INTRODUCTION

I GUESS YOU COULD say I'm a fake, a fraud, a sham. I pretend to be someone I'm not. A lot of people wear masks for a lot of different reasons, but I make a living walking in someone else's shoes.

I am a professional impersonator.

I imitate someone who for eight years was the most powerful man on the planet: the president of the United States of America, our "commander-er" in chief, George W. Bush.

It's the role of a lifetime. (By the way, I've been trying to get Hollywood to shoot the sequel to *Air Force One*. They could call it *Air Force One, Two* and I'll play the role of Harrison Ford.)

I look like the president and can sound like the president. I've imitated him onstage before thousands and on television before millions. I've invaded the Democratic Presidential Campaign headquarters in Boston, freaked out the folks at CNN Headquarters in Atlanta, been cheered by American armed forces generals in Germany, and turned down the opportunity to be spanked by Marilyn Manson's girlfriend in a music video. I've even convinced America's first lady of journalism, Barbara Walters, that I was actually Dubya.

But none of this holds a candle to whom we are all called to imitate: Jesus, the very Son of God.

People often look at me and my outrageous life and say, "Gee, I wish I looked like somebody famous." I have great news for you. If you are a believer in Christ, you do! You have been recreated in the image of God's Son and have His indwelling presence living through you.

Instinctively, we all know that we were born to do more, to be greater than we are, but we often settle for the mundane when the call to real significance rings in our hearts, awakening a longing that can only be satisfied in Christ. Let the truth be told. You were made to be like God. You were created to imitate the life of Jesus Christ and live the greatest adventure imaginable.

This is an adventure book. I have done crazy, outlandish things that most people wouldn't do—and I have succeeded, because by God's grace I trusted and obeyed. But before that, I was a fearful, fractured half-life, someone unable to accept any serious challenge because I believed the lie that I would certainly fail.

Sound familiar? Then come and meet the Truth. His name is Jesus, and He wants you to follow Him, to hear His voice and trust Him. I hope my story encourages you to walk fearlessly like Jesus walked, to obey like Jesus obeyed. God himself has written each chapter of your story, and He is inviting you into the greatest adventure imaginable.

I have the honor of impersonating the president in all kinds of settings. It's a joy to step in and out of character, to be George Bush one moment and to be John Morgan the next.

Many of my performances are for corporate clients, who have hired me to provide a comedic impersonation of our commander in chief. Because they have employed me as an entertainer, it is usually not appropriate for me to step out of character and talk about my faith, but even in these settings, I try to encourage folks to fearlessly pursue their dreams. I've learned that I can leave an indelible impression by the way I treat everyone at the venue, through my commitment to doing my very best, and by serving their needs to the fullest.

As I've made a career of impersonating the president, I've learned that each of us has a choice about whom we emulate. God—in His infinite irony—has used this to change me from a fraud who simply pretends to live into an imitator of God with a life filled with faith and expectancy.

So welcome to my story, *My Life as a Bush...and My Heart for Imitating Jesus.*

Your Presidential Amigo,

JOHN MORGAN

CHAPTER 1

WAKING UP to FIND I'M SOMEONE ELSE

For it is light that makes everything visible. This is why it is said: "Wake up, O sleeper, rise from the dead, and Christ will shine on you."

[EPHESIANS 5:14]

IT WAS WAY past midnight when my wife's voice shook me from a stone dead sleep. Was something wrong with the boys? Had something happened to our aging parents?

I saw Kathy's smile and immediately realized everything was fine. But why would this otherwise sane woman rouse her exhausted husband from his rest? She leaned over, hugged me, and announced, "I've found your new career—impersonating the president!"

This idea wasn't exactly new.

I had been helping set up chairs for Governor George Bush's 2000 presidential campaign in our hometown of Orlando when one of his staffers gawked at me and said, "Did anyone ever tell you that you look like Dubya?" Three years and hundreds of similar comments later, at my mother's eightieth birthday party our friend Paula went on and on about how I should impersonate the president. I immediately rejected the thought. The dark song of my own doubts and fears, my bitter "what if's" and "if only's" had drowned out the call to adventure.

The turning point came in 2003 when Kathy was watching late night TV and saw a comedian imitating Bush and thought, "Hey, John's as good as *that guy*. I wonder how much he makes." She promptly got online and found the Web sites of a couple of prominent Bush impersonators. Her jaw hit the floor when she found out what they earned for a single appearance!

That was the night she woke me up. Not just literally, but figuratively as well.

Up to that point, I had lived an in-the-box existence. In fact, I had defined the box! I had lived in the same town, gone to the same church, and worked for my parents' appliance company most of my life. Change and I were not good friends.

In the eighties I had made a stab at a singing career, but that had fizzled out, along with my dreams of adventure. Kathy and I had married, settled down, and we were raising four sons and whatever menagerie of animals she had adopted each month. Our lives were safe and predictable.

That is, until Kathy's midnight epiphany. Then things changed.

At first, I was convinced that this was a bad idea. I had seen my share of Elvis impersonators and Marilyn Monroe look-alikes. After all, John Morgan was a hard-working, respectable, church-going citizen. I had no desire to join the circus.

This "impersonate the prez" idea was, well, just weird. Still, one of my lifelong prayers had been, "Lord, please don't let me miss Your will." The thought hit me, "What if this is actually God's plan?" I scoffed at the very idea, but decided I'd better pray about it, you know, just in case. I even fasted for two weeks to put myself in a spiritual position to hear His voice.

To my surprise, God said yes!

Like many other people, I have had times when I knew I clearly heard God directing me, speaking to my heart. This was one of them. I knew that I knew. Now I had a choice: to obey or not obey.

I heard a clear calling to leave the safety and predictability of my normal, make-no-waves life to imitate the president of the United States. Sounds a little nuts, doesn't it? As foolish as it seemed, the Lord wanted me to use the face and voice He gave me to impersonate George Bush. He would bless my audiences with laughter, provide for my family, and bring glory to Himself.

It was outrageous, it was scary, and my job was to simply say yes.

The night that Kathy woke me up to my new calling was a defining moment in my career as an impersonator, but it was more than two decades earlier that I personally encountered the Christ I am called to imitate.

Growing up as the youngest of four children, I was cute and fearless. I was a little showman and usually got plenty of attention. As I grew older, this need for applause devolved into a fear of rejection. I would literally do anything for acceptance. As a teenager, I became a walking cliché of the rock-and-roll party lifestyle. I spent many of my teenage years indulging in illegal drugs and sexual immorality. On Sunday morning, I was the fresh-faced kid on the front row at church, but I had spent the night before trying to fill my spiritual emptiness with everything the preacher railed against.

To me, religion was just one more thing I did for acceptance. I was good at keeping the rules, and I was even better at breaking them, depending on whom I was trying to impress. In those days, God was just a concept, not a real person. It was easy to ignore a concept. That was until I met some "Jesus freaks" who seemed to know God personally. Their lives had been changed, and they seemed to have a real peace and joy that I hadn't experienced in all my years of partying. God called to me through their loving imitation of Christ, and I prayed an imperfect prayer, something like, "Lord, if You're real, then please help me. I don't know how You could love someone like me. Right now, I'm not willing to give my life to You, but I am willing to be made willing."

For the next three years, God worked in my life until I finally came to the end of myself and was born again into His family.

God's plan from the beginning of time has been to have deep, intimate fellowship with people who would love Him and reflect His character. That's why we read in Genesis 1:26, "Then God said, 'Let us make man in our image, in our likeness.'" His plan was for us to be like Him. Although sin seemed to thwart His purpose, God loved us too much to let us spend eternity without Him, so He sent His Son to lay down His life for our sins; and He sent His Spirit to actually make His home in every new believer.

We can open our hearts to God's free gift of salvation by confessing our sinfulness and inadequacy without Christ. Then, by faith, we can receive the forgiveness Jesus purchased for us with His own precious blood on the cross and by His resurrection three days later. When we trust Jesus as our Lord and Savior, God makes us new creations, empowering us by His Holy Spirit to live lives that will honor Him.

God's children can be like Him because Jesus now resides in them. This is the secret to living like Jesus: "I have been crucified with Christ and I no longer live, but Christ lives in me. The life I live in the body, I live by faith in the Son of God, who loved me and gave himself for me" (Gal. 2:20).

All of us face choices. But the true defining moment for each of us will be the spiritual crossroads where we decide whether to accept or reject Christ. We can't have it both ways.

This defining moment will change everything forever.

Everyone needs a starting point, and my true life as a Christ impersonator began the day I said yes.

Such a simple word; such a profound change.

The light came on, and this sleeper awoke to find he was someone else.

QUESTIONS *for* REFLECTION

1. What are some of the defining decisions—good or bad—that you have made thus far in your life?

2. Describe some "waking-up" moments that you experienced when the light seemed to come on and the choices before you became clear.

3. The Bible tells us that the first step to being recreated in God's image is to be born anew in the image of Christ. Have you accepted God's gift of salvation? Would you like to? Then simply have a heartfelt talk with God in prayer, confessing your sins and inviting Him to become Lord of your life.

4. If you are a believer in Jesus, have you experienced other turning points where Christ called you into a deeper walk with Him? Could you describe one?

CHAPTER TWO

YOU'RE PUTTING ME ON!

*Put on the new self, created to be like God
in true righteousness and holiness.*

[EPHESIANS 4:24]

Hﾟᴏᴡ ᴅᴏ ʏᴏᴜ begin to impersonate the president of the United States?

George W. Bush regularly wears a dark suit, a white shirt, an American flag lapel pin, and a royal blue tie. I wanted to look like him, so I dressed like him. I combed my hair the way he does. I left my tie-dyed Grateful Dead T-shirt, safari pants, hippie beads, and Birkenstocks in the closet.

The clothes were the obvious part.

Then came the work.

My first thought was to get on the Internet and download some clips of the president. I videotaped him whenever he was on television, and then practiced his posture, his diction, and his hand gestures. I would play a clip of the president, and then I would practice his delivery over and over. My son Daniel, who was thirteen at the time, became my voice

7

coach. We would listen to the president speak, I would try to mimic his accent, and Daniel would point out where I had succeeded and where I just sounded like John Morgan with a cold. I spent hours practicing in front of the mirror and the TV—even listening and repeating phrases in the car with a handheld voice recorder.

Then I bought books about George W. Bush. I read speeches, biographies, and essays about his life and beliefs. I found out what made him tick and what ticked him off. I read what other people wrote about him. I read what he wrote about other people. If I was going to be the best impersonator possible, then I wanted to know WWDD?—What Would Dubya Do?

But that wasn't all. I got back on the Internet and found out everything I could about the impersonation business. I was astounded to discover that there is a whole look-alike industry with its own trade associations, conventions, award shows, and agencies. Then I picked up the phone and began to call some of those folks to seek their advice. I was amazed at the amount of insight, help, and encouragement I received. The look-alike industry is a big, happy family that welcomed me with open arms.

Finally, it was time to go public. That October, a church in our community was hosting a fall festival costume party. I decided to show up as President Bush. I was nervous and self-conscious; I had no idea how it would go. But before I even got in the door, people starting saying, "Hey, look! There's the president!"

It was a blast! I was hooked.

The next opportunity came the following month when I begged my sister, Mary Ann, a prominent Orlando attorney, to let me be a surprise guest at her law firm's Christmas party.

I borrowed a few quips from another impersonator's routine and opened my mouth for the first time in public as our president. Standing there in the hallway before my first real performance, I had that feeling you get at the beginning of a roller coaster ride when the shoulder restraints clamp down and you wonder if this is such a good idea after all. But before I knew it, this normally staid group of lawyers were doubled over in laughter. It was a huge rush and extremely encouraging at the outset of my unlikely journey.

When I look back at the videotapes of my performances during those early days, I can't help but cringe a little. My make-up was amateurish, my accent way off, and my material was corny. Still, I remember the great joy I felt in following my new calling.

To imitate Jesus, we're obviously not talking about donning a fake beard, a bathrobe, and some flip-flops, and going around saying, "Verily, verily." Neither are we talking about a culturally irrelevant religion or a faith that is beyond the reach of the common man. There is nothing fake or hypocritical or irrelevant or untouchable about Jesus.

God made you and me to become just like His Son, and God's Word shows us how.

Paul writes in Ephesians 4 that each of us must consciously abandon our resemblance to anything other than Jesus and intentionally wrap ourselves in the new character that comes from Christ. Establishing new habits and lifestyle patterns can be hard, but the more we count ourselves alive in Jesus, the more easily we can live as "dead to sin" (Rom. 6:11). This renewal of our minds is both a work of the Holy Spirit and an act of our will—and it is all accomplished by God's grace.

Most of us know some really talented musicians or athletes who have been blessed with extraordinary gifts. But for them to really succeed, they must apply themselves to their art or sport. They must study and train and practice and sacrifice. The gift alone is no guarantee of greatness. This same adage applies to our new lives in Christ. Because of His great love, God has blessed us with something we don't deserve. We can keep that gift on the shelf, or we can put it to work for the good of others and the glory of God. Paul writes that laziness is not an option for us.

> Whatever you do, work at it with all your heart, as working for the Lord, not for men, since you know that you will receive an inheritance from the Lord as a reward. It is the Lord Christ you are serving.
> —Colossians 3:23–24

Can you see some of the spiritual parallels in my preparation for impersonation?

First, I committed myself to reading everything I could about the person I was imitating. Then I started making his words mine. Along the way, I had friends and family who encouraged my progress—even offering loving advice and correction. I discovered a whole new family who welcomed me and cheered me as I learned to lay aside my old self and put on my new character.

The Lord has given us a tremendous support system as we strive to imitate His Son. He's given us the Bible to reveal both His character and His plan for our lives. He has put His Holy Spirit in our hearts so that we can have "the mind of Christ" (1 Cor. 2:16). He has invited us into real community with other believers, His church. God has also called us under the authority of pastors and elders who can speak loving truth into our lives.

The Lord is there when we start running the race, there when we stumble, there to help pick us up, and He'll be there cheering when we eventually cross the finish line. Even though He foreknew what we would become, God the Father still takes immeasurable joy in our imitation of the Son He loves, in whom He is perfectly pleased.

QUESTIONS *for* REFLECTION

1. Who are some of the people—living or dead—who have been role models for you thus far in your life?

2. What aspects of their character have you intentionally or unintentionally imitated?

3. Have you ever considered taking on the attributes of Jesus? Based upon your understanding of Scripture, what are some of the characteristics of Christ that you would like to reflect?

4. Likewise, what traits do you possess that you feel are in conflict with Jesus' character? Have you considered asking God to help you put aside these things so that He can recreate His character in you?

CHAPTER THREE

The INAUGURATION of an IMPERSONATOR

> *Now to him who is able to do immeasur-*
> *ably more than all we ask or imagine, according*
> *to his power that is at work within us, to him*
> *be glory in the church and in Christ Jesus*
> *throughout all generations, for ever and ever.*
>
> [EPHESIANS 3:20–21]

GOD HAS BIG plans for us—bigger than we dare to dream!

I wonder if Peter was the only disciple to ever walk on water with Jesus. Perhaps Thomas was invited but demurred, saying, "Oh, I'll just stay here in the boat where I can hold on to this mast."

Sometimes we feign false humility, excusing ourselves with the thought that we're not worthy to be called into such a grand adventure. The truth is that we're *not* worthy, but God delights in doing things through us that we could never do on our own. That way, He gets the glory. If we only accomplished what was within our power to do, then no one would call it miraculous. No one would see His hand at work in our lives.

When I was called to become a professional impersonator, I stepped out of the boat and tried not to look back. It was both exhilarating and terrifying, but there is a simple beauty in obedience. Not questioning, doubting, or analyzing; just believing.

And belief is powerfully contagious. I talked Kathy into donning a Laura Bush-like wig and makeup. I persuaded some friends of ours to let us pose for publicity photos in front of their shiny black limousine. Then I posted our contact information on an imperfect Web site with the perfect URL, georgebushimpersonator.com.

I continued to research this peculiar industry and discovered that the 2004 Sunburst Convention of Celebrity Impersonators and Look-Alikes was meeting right in our hometown of Orlando. We attended and passed out George & Laura Bush business cards there. To our delight, we got a callback for our first big gig in Orlando, for IBM!

We practiced and practiced for that event and felt that we were as ready as we would ever be. As we confidently walked into the hotel with the event planner for the IBM appearance, she casually asked me how long we had been doing this. When I told her that this was our first real professional appearance, she almost had a heart attack! She quickly swore us to secrecy regarding this, which really didn't matter because everyone ended up having a great time. For Kathy and me, this was just more fuel for the fire that the Lord had lit in our hearts.

Little did we know that this was just the beginning of more mind-bending moments for us. The phone began to ring off the hook.

Signature Flight, the world's largest provider of business aviation services, called to see if we were available for an appearance in January 2005...

...in Washington, D.C...

...for President George W. Bush's inauguration!

Our responsibility would be to greet the VIPs who were using their executive jetport the day before and the day after the event. This was more than we could have ever imagined.

After our first day's performance, a limousine was provided to transport us to and from our hotel where the Florida GOP had hired us for a photo session. A limo! Wow! We acted like this was an everyday occurrence, but inwardly we felt like two kids on Christmas morning. Washington, D.C, was absolutely mobbed. As our driver inched through bumper-to-bumper traffic, I would roll down my window a little and tip my hand and wink at the other drivers just enough to sell the illusion. Then, we'd watch from behind our tinted windows as they would try to convince their traveling companions they had just seen the president! Our driver was laughing so hard that I grew genuinely concerned about his ability to maintain control of the vehicle. At one point along our journey, an entire crowd of teenagers chased our limo down the street begging for a picture. Of course, we obliged.

The night before the Republican Party of Florida hosted one of the official inaugural balls they threw a gala reception at our hotel. As part of the lavish decoration, they had turned a gazebo-shaped room inside the hotel into a detailed replica of the Oval Office, complete with presidential carpet, windows, and draperies. As the imitator in chief, I completed the picture. When the reception and photo session began, I had the opportunity to be photographed with and speak to many people who had been with the president. I was very blessed to hear their positive comments and continued posing for photos until the reception ended.

The following day was January 20, 2005: Inauguration Day!

The weather was bitterly cold, and we were dressed for the outdoors. I was asked whether or not I was going to attend the inauguration in costume. "Definitely not," I said. That day was not about me. It was President Bush's day.

Kathy and I joined friends from Florida, along with some new friends we had just made, and plunged into the gargantuan crowd. There were at least three hundred thousand people, if not more; a sea of faces who were all there to participate in history, to catch a glimpse of their president, and to bask in the glory of America. We waited for what seemed like hours to get inside the turnstiles and past the security point near the front of the Capital Building, where we would watch the swearing-in ceremony. No one minded the long lines. There was such unity, joy, and unbridled patriotism. I felt right at home.

That evening, Kathy and I attended the Liberty Ball. Again, I didn't go in character, but because I was dressed in a tuxedo, I couldn't help but look a lot like Dubya. Kathy looked absolutely luminous in her lovely blue gown.

People started snapping pictures left and right. Every so often, folks would turn and gasp as we walked by, convinced that they had just rubbed elbows with the commander in chief. At one point, the crowd had pressed so tightly around us and the cameras were flashing so brightly that I grew a little panicky. It was surreal.

Soon, the Secret Service began to gather around the stage and placed the Presidential Seal on the podium, which is done right before the president speaks. George and Laura Bush emerged to the stirring strains of "Hail to the Chief," looking radiant. The crowd erupted in jubilant applause. The president and the first lady stepped up to the microphone and warmly thanked everyone who helped make this day possible. Then the orchestra struck up a waltz and the first couple treated everyone to an inaugural dance.

Afterward, they excused themselves to repeat this scene at other presidential balls around the city. Holding Kathy close to my side, I drank in every sight and sound, knowing that this was truly a once in a lifetime moment.

We left the ball so late that we missed the last shuttle back to our rooms. Although it was several blocks back to our hotel, we decided to walk anyway. The temperature had plunged even lower, and the frigid air hit us like a wall of ice as we exited the convention center. To make matters worse, Kathy's feet were aching from hours of walking and dancing, so she couldn't wear her shoes. In desperation, she had to hike up the bottom part of her gown so I could carry her piggy back through the frozen streets of Washington. We started laughing at how funny we must have looked and were grateful that no photographers were around. I could just see the picture in tomorrow's tabloids with the caption, "President Bush sneaks shoeless woman in formalwear through D.C. streets on piggyback."

The following morning, we were back at the D.C. Executive Airport in full costume to thank folks for coming and to provide a photo opportunity. I looked down the concourse and saw famed television journalist Barbara Walters, who had interviewed the president the previous evening.

An impish idea hit me, and I immediately grabbed Kathy, who was dressed as Laura Bush. We headed straight for the Walters entourage. As soon as I caught Barbara's eye, she rushed up to me and said, "Mr. President, Mr. President, were you pleased with last night's interview?" It was hard to keep a straight face, but I made that "Bushy squint" with my eyes, reached out, and shook her hand, saying, "Barb'ra, it's soooo good to see ya!"

Later that week on her ABC network show, *The View*, Barbara Walters shared her startling encounter—and that suspension of disbelief that momentarily turns peoples' minds to mush when they first see me: "I realized that this man was a George Bush look-alike—the very image of him. He fooled me!"

What a trip!

In Jeremiah 29:11, we read this promise, "'For I know the plans I have for you,' declares the Lord, 'plans to prosper you and not to harm you, plans to give you hope and a future.'"

God's plans are audacious, miraculous, and compassionate. His purposes cannot fail.

I believe the Lord exists above time itself, so the very concepts of yesterday, today, and tomorrow are meaningless to a God who treats things that haven't happened as if they already had. If God is that confident about our future, then why aren't we?

Because we resist God's call to live by faith.

We don't really trust Him.

Instead, we depend upon our limited senses, our limited knowledge, and our limited experiences.

Real life begins, however, when we choose to believe that faith in God is a far better way to interpret reality than science, logic, or emotions. Hebrews 11:1 says, "Now faith is being sure of what we hope for and certain of what we do not see." Note the words *sure* and *certain*. These are words of supreme confidence. That is why Paul, who constantly faced severe persecution and hardship, defiantly wrote, "If God is for us, then who can be against us?...No, in all these things we are more than conquerors through him who loved us" (Rom. 8:31, 37).

Paul lived fearlessly, trusting that his life had real meaning and that his mission would not fail. He simply trusted God.

So can you and I.

Hey, I know that on the outside I'm just mild-mannered John Morgan, former home appliance salesman from Orlando. But God's Word says that on the inside, I'm being filled to overflowing with the strength, love, power, and character of Christ, so that I can experience a God-sized life.

QUESTIONS *for* REFLECTION

1. What, if anything, keeps you from living the great adventure to which you feel called?

2. Recount some situations where you "stepped out of the boat" and God helped you "walk on water." Have you ever stepped out on faith and failed?

3. Reread Jeremiah 29:11, printed earlier in this chapter. On a scale of 1 to 10, rate how well you feel you are trusting God with your future hopes and dreams.

4. Take a few moments and talk honestly with God about your life. Consider giving Him permission to help you move beyond fear to confidence, if that is your present need and true desire.

CHAPTER FOUR

IMITATION HAPPENS

*Be imitators of God, therefore, as dearly
loved children and live a life of love, just as
Christ loved us and gave himself up for us as
a fragrant offering and sacrifice to God.*

[EPHESIANS 5:1–2]

A LITTLE BOY PUSHES a toy lawnmower as his daddy
does yard work, and a little girl plays dress-up with her mother's makeup and jewelry.

Imitation happens.

Our heavenly Father has woven this ability into our
very DNA. We learn to walk and talk by mimicking those
around us.

Sometimes parents are pleased when their children are their
"spittin' image"—a Southern contraction literally meaning
"spirit and image." Other times we are shocked when our kids
spout out colorful language, only to realize that they learned
these little ditties from us!

Imitation happens automatically, but it also happens by
choice.

My first intentional impersonation was in self-defense.

When I was around seven years old, we were visiting some relatives in nearby St. Petersburg, Florida. While there, my cousin Debbie walked my other cousins and me down to the nearby inner-city park. Without warning, three of the local kids marched over to where I was playing, yanked me off of my swing, and threw me facedown into the dirt. While two of these creeps held me, the other one reached in and stole the entire contents of my pocket—a quarter!

I was scared to death, so I just did what came naturally. I fought back and beat all of them to a bloody pulp.

Yeah, right. Actually, I started to cry.

I was not in much physical pain, but my youthful inno-cence had just been blown to smithereens. One of the boys came over to me and said, "Man, why you crying?"

Call it quick thinking or survival instinct. Whatever the case, I tearfully mimicked his urban accent back to him, telling him that they had taken the only quarter I had ever had. Now this was clearly a lie. It was not my first quarter, nor was it my only quarter. Neither was that my real voice. But the kid went back over and talked to his friends. Out of mercy—or maybe just pity—they gave me back my quarter.

As odd as it sounds, this was a defining moment in my young life.

Victimization had turned to victory!

I ran back to the house and told everyone about the attempted mugging and the remarkable reversal. I had expe-rienced the irresistible power of impersonation, but it wasn't too long before I began to wield this force, as Darth Vader did in *Star Wars*, for the dark side.

As I grew up, I began to use imitation as a coping mecha-nism for deep, personal insecurities. I felt unaccepted and scorned, so I adapted by creating false personalities in order to fit in socially. I was like a chameleon, changing my colors for whatever group I was with. My masks became my cover. I lived in the third person, always second-guessing my conversations. I fought the nagging knowledge that I was a phony, and though I did develop friendships, I feared that those who really got to know me would reject me. I was anything but authentic.

But imitation happens.

As a teenager, I idolized and imitated the most celebrated sinners of my generation. First, it was thrilling, and then it was addictive. I went from being subtly captivated by this behavior to being totally imprisoned by it. Even after Christ saved me from this lifestyle, it took many years for me to be fully delivered from its effects.

Don't be fooled. Sin is like jumping out of an airplane. Once you've jumped out, you can't get back in. There's only one direction to go—down. And if the fall doesn't kill you, that sudden stop at the bottom will.

Several years ago, there was a TV commercial promoting a security monitoring device that older people could wear around their necks. If they had an accident or seizure, they could press a button to call for help. The advertisement depicted an elderly woman who cried, "Help! I've fallen and I can't get up!" That catchphrase is still popular today, usually as part of a joke. But sin is no laughing matter, and the truth is that we are all fallen and can't get up on our own.

God accomplishes what we cannot. In his letter to the church at Rome, Paul wrote, "Don't copy the behavior and customs of this world, but let God transform you into a new person by changing the way you think. Then you will know what God wants you to do, and you will know how good and pleasing and perfect his will really is" (Rom. 12:2, NLT).

When I first came to faith in Christ, I thought my old habits and behaviors would automatically disappear. When they didn't, I simply began to build phony façades for a new batch of people. No one seemed to be struggling with my particular brand of temptations—or at least no one was talking about it. I soon felt alone again. I thought I was the worst person in my church, and that if anyone found out the sin issues I struggled with, they'd run me out of town on a rail.

Over time, I began to understand that every believer is in the process of un-imitating the world, of trading the burden of sin for the freedom of forgiveness, of learning to trust other believers who thought that *their sin* was the worst one out there. The Lord let me see that I have been adopted into a whole new family, where all of us are learning to take off our masks and live authentically.

I learned that was I was not alone, but that it was God's plan all along to put me in the company of fellow former fakers, that God was using my brothers to help strengthen me, and vice versa. Instead of being influenced by people corrupted by rebellion and self-deception, I began taking on the character of men whose passion was to follow Christ authentically.

Hope replaced despair.

Fellowship replaced isolation.

Joy replaced fear.

I am profoundly aware that there are folks reading this who will identify with the pain I experienced.

Dear friend, if that is you, there is great hope in imitation, but not in the phony, cover-up life you may be living. By allowing Christ to live within you and through you, you will experience an authentic new life increasingly marked by *His* character.

You will not only learn how to be forgiven, but how to love

and forgive others as Christ does.

Your fear of exposure will be conquered by your knowledge of God's unconditional acceptance.

You'll begin to see yourself as God sees you—in Christ.

God is at work in us, sanctifying us day by day, transforming us into the image of Jesus. To imitate Christ is to intentionally participate in this change. Imitating the world once brought me darkness and death; imitating Christ now brings me life in all its fullness. Not a bad trade!

QUESTIONS *for* REFLECTION

1. Look back over your life and identify some positive habits and character traits you have learned along the way. Who influenced you? When? How?

2. What kind of negative habits or destructive traits have you acquired? From whom? Was this imitation intentional or unconscious?

3. Have you realized how difficult it is to break the cycle of negative imitation without divine intervention and human encouragement?

4. What choices can you make today that will decrease the sin influence and increase the Spirit influence in your life?

CHAPTER FIVE

WHAT WOULD DUBYA DO?

So Jesus said, "...I do nothing on my own but speak just what the Father has taught me. The one who sent me is with me; he has not left me alone, for I always do what pleases him."

[JOHN 8:28–29]

P<small>EOPLE OFTEN ASK</small> me if I have met George W. Bush, and if so, what he thought about my imitation of him. I *did* meet him once, though I was not in makeup and costume. As he shook my hand in a receiving line, I said, "Mr. President, it's an honor to be your look-alike." He just tilted his head to the side, squinted his eyes, and chuckled, "Well, I feel sorry for ya!"

I love to tell that story, not just because it's funny, but because it gives great insight into President Bush's relaxed, self-deprecating, and humble style. I truly enjoy impersonating a man who is easygoing and friendly, who would rather be right than popular, and who values family and faith. He's also a bit corny, often spontaneous, and doesn't mind being the punch line of a good-humored jab.

I would like to think that the president and I have these things in common, and because we do, imitating him comes very naturally to me. Perhaps that's why so many people have told me that I not only look like Dubya, but that my imitation seems so effortless. I think it's because I am being my real self as I impersonate him.

When I am preparing material for a personal appearance, I find myself asking, what would Dubya do? I am absolutely committed to my impersonation being in character with his. Even though my routines are marked by exaggeration and parody, it would do a disservice to my audience if they lost the sense they were in the presence of the commander in chief.

In fact, I have declined to portray the president in roles that I felt were out of character. For example, early in my career I was approached about being spanked by shock-rocker Marilyn Manson's girlfriend in a music video. Later, I chose to pass up being in a music video for Jurassic 5 (featuring Dave Matthews), where a clueless President Bush jogs through the streets of a major city, indifferent to minorities, environmentalists, illegal aliens, and the unemployed. I was also sent the script for *Harold and Kumar Escape from Guantanamo Bay*, where the two slacker heroes parachute into George W. Bush's Crawford, Texas, ranch and share drugs from the president's private, high-grade stash.

Earlier in my life, I might have jumped at the chance to be irreverent and disrespectful, but I esteem the man I imitate. No matter what I happen to think about any particular aspect of the president's politics, I have chosen to respect his person, his position, and the country that has elected him to the highest office in the land. That's not to say that I don't have fun as I impersonate President Bush, because joy and laughter are some of the gifts I am privileged to leave with my audience. But I will not seek to discredit or ridicule him. If anything, I believe I have the honor of being his ambassador, representing his character among friends and foes alike.

Likewise, as imitators of Christ, we are called to live in character, taking care to represent Him with joy and integrity.

Even Jesus, the very image of His heavenly Father, defined His own mission as doing and saying only what His Father had taught Him to do and say (John 8:28). Christ does not obey God because He fears retribution or punishment; rather, He loves His Father so much that he said, "I always do what pleases him" (John 8:29). Christ does nothing in His own power or for His own benefit. His motivation is upward toward His Father and outward towards those His Father has sent Him to seek and save. Jesus is always "in character," embodying His Father's love.

> As the Father has loved me, so have I loved you. Now remain in my love. If you obey my commands, you will remain in my love, just as I have obeyed my Father's commands and remain in his love. I have told you this so that my joy may be in you and that your joy may be complete. My command is this: Love each other as I have loved you. Greater love has no one than this, that he lay down his life for his friends. You are my friends if you do what I command... This is my command: Love each other.
>
> —John 15:9–14, 17

Christ's love toward you and me is as vast and eternal as it can possibly be. Take a deep breath and bask in the love of the Father. He clearly has His eyes on you, watching and caring deeply about your every need. His forgiveness is ultimate and complete, and His affection for you will never change, because it is based on His unconditional love for you and not upon your faithfulness to Him.

So how can we live and love like Jesus?

We can't, unless we are truly rooted and grounded in Him. Christ clearly explains, "I am the vine; you are the branches. If a man remains in me and I in him, he will bear much fruit; apart from me you can do nothing" (John 15:5). The only way we can do what the Father wants us to do is to be so vitally connected to Christ that we naturally do what He does. Likewise, I've found that trying to accomplish anything within my own power and solely for my own benefit leads to failure.

It seems that God delights in reminding me of this last fact.

During the 1980s, I believed that the Lord wanted Kathy and me to share our stories of how He redeemed our lives and gave us a faith-filled marriage and family. We called our ministry "Love Works" and performed wherever we could. I recorded a couple of custom albums during that time and tried unsuccessfully to pursue a national recording deal with some Christian music companies in Nashville. Looking back, I can now joke that I lacked two key ingredients for success: talent and integrity. But seriously, folks, I truly believe the Lord knew I wasn't ready for such responsibility. I eventually set aside that dream to focus on being a faithful husband, father, church member, and employee in our family appliance business. I was learning the meaning of Psalm 46:10: "Cease striving and know that I am God" (NAS). I was learning to abide in the vine; learning to find my identity, security, and strength in Christ alone.

Years passed by. My sons grew older. Some went to college. One got married. After the Gardener had pruned and dressed and prepared my branches, I was finally ready to bear His fruit for the whole world to see.

What I had been unable to accomplish in years of striving, God did in a matter of days.

It started with an inquiry to my web site from New Haven Records, a Christian music company in Nashville. No, they didn't want to sign me to a recording contract. Rather, they wanted me to be the celebrity host for their portion of a national sales conference. Their marketing consultant, Vince Wilcox, worked with me to craft the comedic script for the presentation.

I flew into Nashville first thing Thursday morning, rehearsed the show around lunchtime, and then made the presentation early that afternoon.

The show rocked! We had several guys decked out in full Secret Service regalia. "Hail to the Chief" blared through a sound system worthy of a music company's national sales conference, and as they say, the crowd went wild! Afterward, I was told that this was their most unforgettable presentation *ever*.

Vince and I spoke at length later that afternoon, striking up what has turned into a deep and vibrant friendship. (At the moment of this writing, Vince and I are video-conferencing about this chapter and actually waving to you from the soul of this book. Hey, it's my book—I can be weird if I wanna!)

At the end of our conversation, I asked him if he and his business partner, Troy VanLiere, might consider managing me. He responded that it would be a few weeks before they would be able to discuss this possibility because Vince and his wife were leaving the following Monday on a cruise.

I asked him if it happened to be The Music Boat Cruise,

departing out of Miami. Amazingly enough, it was!

I had heard about the cruise because Stephen Mansfield, author of *The Faith of George W. Bush*, was scheduled to speak on the ship, which was filled with Christians wanting to be inspired by contemporary Christian music, encouraging speakers, and the glory of God's creation. Unknown to Vince, I had already tried to wrangle my way onboard to meet Stephen.

Since I was not running short on audacity, I then asked Vince if he he could get Kathy and me on The Music Boat. Remarkably enough, Vince and Troy worked closely with The Premier Group, who hosted the cruise. Vince called them on Friday, and by Saturday Premier Christian Cruises had offered us a cabin in exchange for me making a surprise presidential appearance that Monday night.

God synchronized all the details perfectly. By the time the cruise was over, the Lord had blessed me with a manager, a PR firm, and a booking agency to coordinate my appearances. And I got to meet Stephen Mansfield.

Cool story, huh?

If that's what God can accomplish in one week for a comedic impersonator, just imagine what He can do in our families, churches, schools, and workplaces when we learn to abide in Him!

Imagine what would happen if we were always "in character," if everything we did and said was no more and no less than what pleased the Father.

That's God's plan, and He's stickin' to it.

QUESTIONS *for* REFLECTION

1. Reflect on at least one situation where your own best efforts were insufficient to accomplish something that was important to you.

2. Reflect on at least one example where living and abiding in God's will accomplished something in your life that you could never have accomplished on your own.

3. God says to us in Psalm 46:10, "Cease striving and know that I am God" (NAS). When you read this verse, is there one particular area of your life that comes to mind where trusting God needs to replace activity and striving? If so, would you consider committing that area to Christ right now?

4. The best place to begin discovering what Jesus would do are the four short biographies of His life written by His friends and followers. They are located at the beginning of the New Testament section of the Bible. Consider making a daily appointment with Jesus and these Gospels to get to know Him better.

Chapter Six

LEARNING FROM the MAN in the MIRROR

Anyone who listens to the word but does not do what it says is like a man who looks at his face in a mirror and, after looking at himself, goes away and immediately forgets what he looks like. But the man who looks intently into the perfect law that gives freedom, and continues to do this, not forgetting what he has heard, but doing it—he will be blessed in what he does.

[James 1:23–25]

There are more than fifty muscles in the human face, and I bet you never thought about exercising a single one of them the last time you were at the gym.

It wasn't until I got serious about impersonating that I realized the amazing flexibility of our lips, eyebrows, and foreheads. The mirror became my teacher. I would tape a photo of President Bush to it and then put my own face right beside his image, spending hours trying to make every muscle mimic Dubya's.

It was fun. It was frustrating. It was fantastic.

The more I worked at it, the easier it became. In time, I could transform from John to George in the literal blink of an eye or the simple shrug of the shoulders. Then I started working on his voice and mannerisms by watching video after video. The more I practiced, the more like him I became.

My plan was simple: be more like him, be less like me.

Not surprisingly, this is the same attitude that John the Baptist expressed about Jesus: "He must become greater; I must become less" (John 3:30). Perhaps you've heard Michelangelo's famous quote about how he sculpted his masterpieces: "I saw the angel in the marble and carved until I set him free." Much of the Christian life is about chipping away the nonessential stuff that builds up around our hearts over the course of our lives so that Jesus might be plainly seen in us.

I have to agree with James, the author of the New Testament letter bearing his name, that looking in the mirror is a critical part of the process. James wrote that the man after God's heart looks intently into God's Word to experience "the perfect law that gives freedom" (James 1:25). He then lets that image burn into his consciousness and intentionally acts upon what he has seen. In that reflection, we see who Christ really is, who we are without Him, and what we can be in Christ. Looking in the mirror of God's Word compels us to conform ourselves to His character.

Likewise, James wrote that we are just deceiving ourselves if we ignore what we have seen and walk away without making the changes God requires. The Christian life involves real change.

Those who have truly experienced God's extravagant love will not want to settle for the petty, self-centered lifestyles they once lived. As a friend of mine says, "God loves and accepts us just the way we are, but He loves us too much to allow us to stay that way." In his letter to the believers at Corinth, the apostle Paul compared discipleship with the single-minded self-discipline of a star athlete.

> All athletes practice strict self-control. They do it to win a prize that will fade away, but we do it for an eternal prize. So I run straight to the goal with purpose in every step. I am not like a boxer who misses his punches. I discipline my body like an athlete, training it to do what it should.
> —1 Corinthians 9:25–27, NLT

Real impersonation takes real work, but it is well worth the sacrifice.

I count it an honor every time someone comes up to me and says, "Your imitation of President Bush is amazing!" In 2005 and 2007, my peers at the annual Sunburst Convention of Celebrity Impersonators and Look-Alikes awarded me their Mirror Image Award for bearing the closest natural resemblance to the person I imitate. That meant a lot to me.

But I am even more thrilled when someone says, "I see Jesus in you." What a privilege to be Christ's image bearer! The Gospels describe Him as compassionate, loving, righteous, truthful, humble, and self-sacrificial—just like His heavenly Father. That's *what* I want to be, and that's *who* I want to be.

The earliest believers weren't actually called Christians. Rather, they were called "followers of the Way" or "disciples of the Nazarene." Acts 11:26 records that they were first called Christians in Syrian Antioch, a fairly large and very worldly city of about 750,000 people. Most scholars think that the term *Christian* wasn't used before A.D. 59, almost a quarter of a century after Jesus' resurrection. It is also widely believed that *Christian*—implying "little Christs"—was a nickname that the pagans used to mock the early believers, but it's no wonder that the name stuck! What the culture considered a put-down, the early believers considered the highest compliment. What an honor to be called a little image bearer, to stand in such godly contrast to their world that those around them had to take note.

Their imitation of Christ caused them to be noticed, but it also caused them to be blessed. James 1:25 promises that the person who sets himself to the high calling of Christ will be "blessed in all he does."

What does it mean to be blessed? It seems like such a "holy" word, and it is, because the source of blessing is God Himself. The Bible describes being blessed as a profound joy and satisfaction that comes from God. It is not related to our outward circumstances, what is happening around us. We call that "happiness." As odd as it seems, God can bless us through material abundance or in extreme deprivation. He can bring deep, abiding peace in the quiet of a daily devotional or in the midst of overwhelming chaos, and while blessing is not earned, it must be received. We cannot receive God's blessings with our hands clasped in indifference or our fists clinched in rage. Paul told the church at Philippi the secret to living a blessed life:

> Not that I speak from want, for I have learned to be content in whatever circumstances I am. I know how to get along with humble means, and I also know how to live in prosperity; in any and every circumstance I have learned the secret of being filled and going hungry, both of having abundance and suffering need. I can do all things through Him who strengthens me.
> —Philippians 4:11–13, nas

Paul lived—and died—for the joy and privilege of knowing Jesus and being transformed by Him. He had discovered the profound satisfaction of allowing God to empower his attitudes and actions. Paul's imitation of Christ was so persuasive that the believers he mentored were eventually called "little Christs."

The guy obviously spent a lot of time looking into the mirror of God's Word and being transformed both inwardly and outwardly.

QUESTIONS *for* REFLECTION

1. Consider how much time and attention you commit weekly to looking into the mirror of God's Word and allowing His truth to profoundly transform you. Are you satisfied with your progress? What could help you in this process?

2. If you are a believer in Jesus, can you look back and see how Christ is becoming a bigger part of your life as your own desires and plans are being submitted to His will? Reflect on one or two significant examples of this.

3. Have you allowed Christ's character to shine through you so much that people in your world have noticed what's different about you? Consider a recent example.

4. How have you begun to experience God's profound joy and satisfaction—His blessing—as you have set yourself to the self-discipline of being Spirit-led?

CHAPTER SEVEN

JETER and JEERS

If the world hates you, keep in mind that it hated me first. If you belonged to the world, it would love you as its own. As it is, you do not belong to the world, but I have chosen you out of the world. That is why the world hates you.

[JOHN 15:18–19]

IT NEVER OCCURRED to me that being a comedic impersonator might actually be hazardous to my health, but it seems that whenever I'm in character, I become a target for people who don't like President Bush.

I once slipped into the lobby of Madame Tussaud's Wax Museum in Manhattan and, just for fun, struck a pose beside the life-sized figure of New York Yankee superstar Derek Jeter. Minutes later, a woman wearing a Boston Red Sox jersey came in, scoffed at Jeter, and then pretended to choke the neck of what she thought was a wax figure of President Bush. I looked right at her and exclaimed in my best President Bush voice, "Now why would you do that?" Her startled scream caused all the watching tourists in the hall to burst into laughter!

Another time, I was standing outside of The Venetian Resort-Hotel-Casino in Las Vegas when a big, hairy guy started lashing out against my incarnation of George Bush. He kept screaming, "If you want our kids to go to war, then why don't you send your twin daughters to Iraq!" His verbal tirade was loud and aggressive until his wife came over and hauled him away.

When I was in Boston during the 2004 presidential campaign, an anti-Republican drunk chased me through Faneuil Hall Square shouting insults at (who he thought was) the president, until he stumbled on a cobblestone and fell flat on his face. I went back and helped him up, and suddenly I was his new best friend.

In a hotel lobby in Lexington, Kentucky, a well-dressed, professional woman came up to me and commented, "Thanks for ruining the country." I couldn't help but ask her if she were struggling financially, and she responded that she was doing very well. I had to wonder why an otherwise intelligent person would take the time to insult someone who was obviously a celebrity impersonator.

My favorite incident happened at a charity birthday roast in Los Angeles. A well-known movie actress strolled up to me and said, "Since you're not really the president, can I insult you to your face?"

I wish you could see for yourself the intensity with which people respond to being in the presence of an imitator of George W. Bush.

First, there is the powerful illusion of actually being with the president of the United States. It seems like folks are willing to suspend reality for the semblance of meeting the most powerful man in the world. I have actually had people weep uncontrollably and laugh hysterically in my presence. It can be unnerving.

But people also react viscerally to the personality and beliefs of the man himself. President Bush has pursued a policy of expanding democracy across the world. He has acted on the premise that a nation as great as America cannot tolerate governments that terrorize their own citizens. He clearly understands that radical Islam will never shake hands in peace with the Christian West. He believes that right and wrong are not determined by this morning's polls but by a Creator who sets timeless standards by which His creation ought to live.

Admittedly, George Bush can be stubborn, irreverent, and tongue-tied. But the highest job in our land is also the hardest job in the world. It is literally impossible to please all of America's nearly three hundred million citizens all of the time, and almost as impossible to please some of them some of the time.

In our cynical media culture, Dubya's latest malapropisms are instantly beamed to the whole world via YouTube. Late night talk show host David Letterman lampoons him daily in a feature called "Great Moments in Presidential Speeches."

People seem to love or hate George W. Bush, with little in between. There is such animosity for him in the world at large that my friends are actually concerned for my safety, especially when I perform out of the country. They ask me, "Aren't you afraid that some lunatic or terrorist who hates the president will take a shot at you?" (To be honest with you, it wouldn't bug me that much as long as they used imitation ammunition.)

We all know that any time you stand up for something, you'll immediately create an opponent, or even an enemy.

The question is whether that will prevent you from standing strong when it's time to take sides. And make no mistake, there will be a time when each of us must take a stand.

When I was younger, I lacked the courage to choose a side, much less take a stand. Part of my problem was that I could usually empathize with either position in an argument, but the bigger issue was that I was afraid to alienate anyone by disagreeing with them. I cared far more about pleasing people than obeying God. However, as a follower of Jesus, I am learning to play to an audience of One. I am realizing that I don't have to fear the rejection of men since I have received the unconditional acceptance of heaven. When Christ made me a new creation, He gave me a backbone as well.

As an impersonator of the president, I have been jeered because of what he stands for. As a image bearer of Jesus Christ, I can expect no less.

In John 15, Jesus told His followers to expect to be hated by the world. Although *hate* seems such a harsh word, the reality is that each of the twelve disciples—except Judas, who hung himself, and John, who was exiled to the island of Patmos— were persecuted and eventually executed for their faith in Christ.

So what is "the world," and why does it hate Christ and His followers?

First of the all, when the Bible speaks of "the world," it is not referring to our planet. Nor is it talking about the people that God sent His Son to save. God made our beautiful world and loves its inhabitants.

Rather, *the world* is a biblical term used to describe the spiritually evil system that has enslaved Creation from the time of Adam's fall until the moment of Christ's resurrection. As the Apostle Paul writes, "For our struggle is not against flesh and blood, but against the rulers, against the authorities, against the powers of this dark world and against the spiritual forces of evil in the heavenly realms" (Eph. 6:12). In short, it is any attitude or action that has not been surrendered to God's sovereignty.

For the time being, "the world" is at odds with God's kingdom. In truth, the issue was settled two thousand years ago on a crucifixion hill outside the city limits of Jerusalem. "The world" is not long for this world. The clock is ticking. The Bible states that one day Christ will return, and "the God of peace will soon crush Satan under your feet" (Rom. 16:20).

The only thing holding back the tide of judgment is God's mercy, extended so that more people could come to know Christ in the days and hours that remain. Jesus gave His followers a heads-up on what would happen so we wouldn't be fearful: "I have told you these things, so that in me you may have peace. In this world you will have trouble. But take heart! I have overcome the world" (John 16:33).

So what are we to do when we find ourselves in conflict with our world because of our faith in Christ?

The answer is strikingly simple.

In the sixth chapter of Luke's Gospel, Jesus tells us that we are to imitate the character of God: "Be merciful, just as your Father is merciful" (Luke 6:36). Christ tells us to return love for hatred (v. 27), blessings for curses (v. 28), peace for violence (v. 29), and charity for larceny (v. 30). In this way, those in the world will realize that we are not of this world.

They will see in us the same Jesus who looked down from the cross on the very men who tortured and crucified Him and asked His Father to forgive them.

When our lives reflect God's love, the Lord can even use our persecution for His glory. Did you know that more Christians have been martyred for their faith in the past century than in all the previous centuries combined?[1] As we draw closer and closer to the Day of the Lord, the conflict between the kingdom of this world and the kingdom of God will rise to a fever pitch, but for the believer whose life in hidden in Christ, there is nothing at all to fear. Rather, we can take heart and keep imitating Jesus, for He has overcome the world!

---

1 "20th Century Saw 65% of Christian Martyrs, Says Author," Zenit.org (May 10, 2002), http://zenit.org/article-4369?l=english.

QUESTIONS *for* REFLECTION

1. If you are a believer in Christ, has your imitation of Him ever come in conflict with your culture? Your friendships? Your job? Your education? If so, how?

2. When it comes to representing Christ, sometimes Christians are their own worst enemy. How have you found this to be true in your life or the lives of those around you?

3. Perhaps unbelievers are confused by Christians who are undiscernibly similar in actions and attitudes to their neighbors in the world. What differences should mark the life of a Christ-follower?

4. How can our loving response to criticism or persecution actually help communicate the message of the gospel?

My early years as a Bush

Punking America's first lady of journalism, Barbara Walters, at Bush's 2005 inauguration

A providential meeting with author Stephen Mansfield on the Music Boat Cruise

Where it all began, the Sunburst Celebrity Impersonator's Convention

Appliance-salesman-turned-president with body-builder-turned-governor

G. W. takes Manhattan with Kathy and two of our sons, Christopher and Stephen, as Secret Service—Times Square 2005

Can anybody let me in? I locked my keys in Air Force One!

On the set of the ultimate
(alternate) reality show!

With my good buddy,
impersonator Dale Leigh

Chillin' backstage with
multi-platinum music legend
Kirk Franklin

Backstage with Kathy at the 2006 Gospel Music Association Dove Awards

Messing with the minds of the world's largest cable news network

I got punked at my surprise 50th birthday party by Kathy, Mom Eileen, Daddy Chuck, and sisters Janice, Mary Ann, and Becky

Surprise Mexican getaway for me and my first lady

With Crystal Cathedral
pastor Robert A. Schuller
at the Los Cabos Children's
Foundation Benefit

Sunrise over Los Cabos—you just
had to be there

Live in New York on
The Tony Danza Show

The Today Show's Al Roker
wonders "weather"
I'm the real deal

Playing my legendary
McPherson guitar at
Nashville's legendary Tootsie's

With fellow Winter Jam performers NewSong, Stephen Curtis Chapman,
Hawk Nelson, Jeremy Camp, and others

Backstage with Freedom Alliance
founder, journalist, and hero Lt. Col.
Oliver North (USMC, Ret.)

Touring *The Great Debate* with
Hillary Clinton impersonator
extraordinaire Teresa Barnwell

Greeting the 2008 Republican Presidential contenders

Rudy Giuliani

Mitt Romney

Fred Thompson

Mike Huckabee

The president's brother, Governor Jeb Bush, asks me, "Is that you, brother?"

Backstage at Sean Hannity's Freedom Concert in San Diego with country legend Lee Greenwood and Christian pop singer Michael W. Smith

Larry the Cable Guy gives me tips
on how to "Git-R-Done"

Preparing for a fly over the
Rock the Desert Festival,
where I was slated to speak

George Bush grew up in this house.
How I miss the early days of his childhood.

I had the honor of introducing former U.S. Attorney
General John Ashcroft to the 2006 International
Christian Booksellers Convention in Denver

Secret Service deployed to deflect Dubya Donut calorie threat. The president's were glazed.

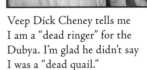

The Prez pumps up with Hans and Franz at the Starlight Theatre in Kansas City

Veep Dick Cheney tells me I am a "dead ringer" for the Dubya. I'm glad he didn't say I was a "dead quail."

An answer to prayer, a dream come true

My wife Kathy looks
like the first lady.
What are the odds?

On the set with *Family Feud*
host John O'Hurley

Top row: John, Kathy, Stephen, Emily, Christopher
Bottom row: Shelby, Daniel, Jonathan, Finley

CHAPTER EIGHT

The ESSENCE of HIS PRESENCE

A new command I give you: Love one another.
As I have loved you, so you must love one
another. By this all men will know that you
are my disciples, if you love one another.

[JOHN 13:34–35]

THERE ARE PERKS for being Dubya's double.

Kathy and I were in New York City in 2005 and decided to go in character to visit the Empire State Building. Flanked by our two oldest sons dressed as Secret Service agents, we walked into the lobby of this great American landmark. The building's manager saw us, started laughing, and said, "Let's go have some fun!" He promptly escorted us past the waiting crowds and into the private elevator that took us directly to the observation deck, where hundreds of visitors from around the world were enjoying the breathtaking panorama of Manhattan. An hour—and oodles of snapshots later—the manager was pleased that he had given his tourist guests an afternoon they would never forget. He thanked us by blessing our whole family with tickets to any Broadway show we wanted to see later that evening.

In 2006, I was invited to be the surprise guest for Youth Day, an annual event produced by Holland's national television network. The concert sponsors wanted to create the illusion that George Bush was actually visiting their arena, so we drove up in a huge motorcade of black limousines escorted by real police on motorcycles. By the time I stepped onstage with my detachment of "Secret Service" agents, the crowd of thirty-five thousand young people were screaming and cheering so loudly I couldn't hear myself stutter. Even after I revealed that I was just a "priceless imitation" of the real thing, I enjoyed the love that I was given on behalf of the president.

I've been given free lattes from Starbucks, an awesome bomber jacket from a U.S. military group in Fort Benning, Georgia, and the remarkable McPherson acoustic guitar I play onstage.

Perhaps the most poignant example of being loved on his account happened to me one day when we were visiting Washington, D.C. I thought it would be fun to stand—totally "Bushified"—right in front of the White House fence and wait to see what would happen. I had barely counted to fifteen when I was swarmed by a huge crowd. An older Asian woman took my hand and thanked me profusely in very broken English for all the blessings that she and her family had received since they immigrated to America. Her thanksgiving was so heartfelt and emotional that all I could do was say, "You're welcome."

In character as President Bush, I have been the beneficiary of love that I never deserved. It's a lot of fun and even humbling at times, but I know that I'm not him. In a far more profound way, because of Jesus, we are the recipients of God's undeserved love.

As a child, I felt unworthy of anyone's love, even the affection of my parents. Because of the years of rejection I encountered at school, I came to believe the negativity I was being fed. I became unable to receive the love my parents offered, and I built walls of protection around my heart. For years I never cried.

As a rebellious teenager, the depth of my depravity further convinced me that no one could ever love me. I've heard it said that while mercy means that we don't get what we really deserve, grace means getting what we don't deserve.

Meeting my wife was a milestone of God's grace in my life. She was a new believer, recently delivered by God's grace from her own history of self-destruction. Kathy and I had two things in common: we both thought that we were unworthy of love, and we both had been redeemed by the mercy of God.

We are all the recipients of a love we do not deserve.

Before the first sunrise in Eden, the infinite God had already committed His Son to a cross on our behalf. Before the first fruit ripened, the first eagle soared, and the first man gazed into the eyes of the first woman, the Lord had it in His mind to redeem us from sins we had not yet been born to commit.

In his letter to the church at Ephesus, Paul used verbs like *chose*, *predestined*, and *adopted* to communicate God's unwavering passion for you and me.

> For he chose us in him before the creation of the world to be holy and blameless in his sight. In love he predestined us to be adopted as his sons through Jesus Christ, in accordance with his pleasure and will—to the praise of his glorious grace, which he has freely given us in the One he loves.
>
> —Ephesians 1:4–6

Every benefit of God's love is assured because we are in Christ, and God can no more deny His Son than He can deny Himself. When God the Father looks at you, Jesus is right beside you with His arm around your shoulder saying, "Dad, this one's with me."

Our sinful rebellion did not negate His love.

Our best efforts cannot earn His love.

Our worst circumstances will not deter His love.

For a professional impersonator, nothing is more important than discovering—and then delivering—the "essence" of the one you are imitating. Sure, there are celebrated lines you can repeat or famous moves you can make, but that's not the same thing as presenting that core attribute.

Christ left absolutely no doubt that love was the essence of His life and that love would be the defining characteristic of anyone who chose to imitate Him.

The night that Jesus was betrayed, He shared a last supper with His followers. He knew that His sacrifice would finally achieve what the Law and the commandments were never able to accomplish: to make true, God-image bearers out of fallen, broken humans. So, knowing that His final words that evening would echo through their hearts eternally, Jesus left His friends with one simple rule: "A new command I give you: Love one another. As I have loved you, so you must love one another. By this all men will know that you are my disciples, if you love one another" (John 13:34–35).

Love.

The essence of His presence.

The defining attribute of His character.

The power that will persuade every onlooker.

The one thing that every God-imitator must practice so that one day the Father will say, "Well done, my child."

QUESTIONS *for* REFLECTION

1. What are some specific instances in your life where you were the recipient of love that you did not deserve?

2. How has that experience transformed you and caused you to become a giver of unconditional love?

3. How can the knowledge of God's eternal, unconditional love for you empower you to love with confidence and grace?

4. Who has the Lord put in your world to be the recipient of your undeserved love and compassion?

CHAPTER NINE

WINNING WHILE LOSING

*Do you see a man skilled in his work? He will serve
before kings; he will not serve before obscure men.*

[PROVERBS 22:29]

Hmmm, let's see.

Do I want to be on a reality show in front of millions of
people? Absolutely! After all, if I don't stink, it'll be good
for business.

The top prize: $100,000.00!

Second prize: all the granola bars you can eat while you're
on the set.

Bea Fogelman, affectionately known as the "Queen Bee"
of the impersonator industry, circulated news that a major
network was working on a reality show for celebrity impersonators. I was interested. Being on a show like this can be
a major commitment of time and reputation, so I called my
friend Greg Thompson, who runs the Sunburst Convention,

to ask for advice. Greg thought I would do well on the show, so I threw my hat into the ring, along with my best buddy in this industry, fellow presidential impersonator Dale Leigh.

Kathy and I first saw Dale while boarding the plane as we were coming home from an event in Chicago. He was standing right in front of us, looking for all the world like Bill Clinton. Kathy couldn't keep it in and exclaimed, "Wow! This is the first time I've ever stood between two presidents!" Dale turned around, gave us a look that would curdle fresh milk, and then put on those wrap-around sunglasses that shout, "Leave me alone!"

When our flight arrived in Orlando and we got to baggage claim, I just couldn't help myself. I tapped Dale on the shoulder, dropped into character, and told him, "Hey amigo, you're missin' out on a lot of fun!" Dale's thin veneer instantly dissolved into a wide smile and laughter.

After about twenty minutes of chatting, we found out that Dale had spent the last decade hating his resemblance to the former president. As Kathy and I shared how much fun we have had—and the monetary rewards we have enjoyed—Dale began to warm up to the idea that his "curse" might actually be a blessing in disguise. We helped convince him to take the plunge. Dale tweaked his natural gifts, learned to play the saxophone, and debuted his Bill Clinton impersonation at the Sunburst Convention—only ten short weeks after we met! Since that providential encounter, Dale and I have become close, personal friends who share a relationship with Christ and a desire to see others transformed by His grace.

Dale flew down from Chicago to Orlando to audition with me at Disney's MGM Studios (now Disney's Hollywood Studios).

The audition went like this: each contestant entered a

sound stage, where the lovely host of the show would interview you. Then, you stepped into an empty room where the three judges held court. There was no audience, only the judges. Each contestant had ninety seconds to audition, unless the judges got what they needed before then.

Right before it was my turn to go on, I felt impressed to pray for the Elvis Presley impersonator sitting to my left. His name was Trent Carlini, and I simply asked God to help Trent do his very best.

Days before, I had called my friend, David Born, a terrific Robin Williams impersonator, for advice. He had already auditioned for the show in Los Angeles. David suggested I start my impression the very moment I entered the room, before I ever reached the microphone. So, I had planned to walk in singing—in Dubya's voice—these lyrics to the tune of "Hail to the Chief": "Dick Cheney hates me; he wants to take me hunting." When the moment of truth arrived, they opened the door. I walked out on stage, but what came out of my mouth was, "Dick Cheney *loves* me; he wants to take me hunting." I thought, "Man! I've already messed up!" I didn't realize until later that I had actually goofed into an even better line.

The audition went very well, and I moved up to the next level.

Not so hot for Dale, but hey, he was new in the business.

Afterward, we went out to dinner at Wolfgang Puck's at Pleasure Island. Dale and I were beset by a restaurant full of tourists who just *had to have* their pictures taken with us. We found out that many of these folks had been in town for a major digital communications convention. The next morning's closing keynote would feature speeches by none other than George H. W. Bush and William Jefferson Clinton themselves!

We scored passes to the trade show and sat spellbound as we experienced elegant, inspiring speeches by these two history-making men. Then, with a little help from some of the *real* Secret Service guys, we worked our way as close as we could to Bush and Clinton. Just as we got within a few steps of the former presidents, they were whisked away in golf carts to their next appointments. Even though we never made eye contact with them, it was enough for us to stand in the same place and breathe the same air.

The semifinals took place in Los Angeles. There were two Elvises, two Robin Williamses, two Dubyas, a Lucy, a Tina, a Streisand, a Sinatra, a Little Richard, a Howard Stern, and other assorted stars, both living and dead. This round was attended by audience members from around L.A., as well as by guests of the performers.

Kathy and I are members of Metro Life Church in Orlando, Florida, which we have attended for over twenty years. Metro Life is affiliated with Sovereign Grace Ministries, a family of churches passionate about the gospel of Jesus Christ. One of our sister churches, Sovereign Grace Church of Pasadena, was located near enough to the venue for some of their folks to come out and cheer me on.

The semi-finals would be taped over a two-day period and would constitute several weeks' worth of episodes. As I walked out onto the stage for my semi-final performance, I was greeted by a friendly, cheering crowd.

But mixed in was something I had not anticipated— booing!

Whether they were jeering the real President Bush or harassing me because I was competing against their friends or family members, it didn't matter. The clock was ticking, and I had to press forward.

Sometimes life is like that. We have to make quick decisions in the moment, with no do-overs. That's why it's so important to spend time in prayer. When I pray, I ask God to prepare me for life's surprises, so that when they come, I will make decisions that glorify Him.

I began my routine, and the crowd started laughing. Even the boo-birds started to join in the laughter. I discovered that it's virtually impossible for someone to boo and laugh at the same time. One judge had even told me, "You're the smarter, better, funnier version of George Bush." Ultimately, the performance won my advancement to the final round!

Something else happened during my stay in Los Angeles. My mom had recently been diagnosed with cancer, and she was hospitalized just before I left Orlando. Although no one thought her condition was immediately life threatening, it was serious enough that I considered dropping out of the competition. After conversations with my family, I made the difficult decision to continue.

The night before the performance, Mom took a turn for the worse. I spent the evening with my friends from the church in Pasadena, praying for her.

At four in the morning, I got a call from my father. "Mom's not going to make it," he said.

I couldn't believe what I was hearing. My mother had been put on life support, and all I could think about was getting home to be with my family.

Dad said, "You can't come home." I sat listening in disbelief as he continued, "Your sisters and I are in agreement. You went there to accomplish something, and Mom would want you to stay. We want you to stay and do it. We need you to do it."

Later that morning, I spoke to Mom one last time via the

speakerphone in her hospital room. I hope she heard me say good-bye and that I loved her. We all sang to Mom, with me on the phone and everyone else in the room. We wondered if she was already gone from this world.

It hurt not to be there, not to be able to hug her or even see her. But I knew Mom, and she truly believed that the moment her spirit was absent from her body she would be in the presence of her Savior. She taught me about faith; and her influence in my spiritual life never waned. Mom was a powerful example of love-motivated obedience and trust. If God led her to witness to someone, she wouldn't rest until she had. Dozens were healed, saved, and delivered through her faith-filled prayers. We became best friends through the years we worked together at our family appliance store, and I pray that I can have the same godly impact on my children and community that she had.

I cried a lot that night and the next day, even as I prepared to compete. My precious wife, Kathy, boarded the first available flight to L.A. so she could be by my side.

Because I wanted to be judged on merit and not on sympathy, I didn't share my loss with the judges or the live national TV audience.

God helped me to perform that night; I just know it. And I felt like Mom was watching from a ringside seat as I gave the performance of my life.

We returned home to Orlando, awaiting the time we would return to L.A. for the finals. The live, televised performance was to be voted on by all of America.

Talk about pressure. Only ten contestants left.

I wanted my final appearance to surprise and amaze everyone, so I played my guitar and danced in character that night. Everyone who knows the story of Moses has heard about the burning bush. That night, I introduced America to the Singing Bush.

"Wow! Wow! Wow! Wow! Wow! Incredible! Incredible!" Those were the first words out of one judge's mouth following my performance.

Even though I lost my Mom during my experience on the show, God's grace had sustained and empowered me. Like the psalmist sang, "You have turned my mourning into joyful dancing. You have taken away my clothes of mourning and clothed me with joy, that I might sing praises to you and not be silent. O LORD my God, I will give you thanks forever" (Ps. 30:11–12).

Well, the rest of the story is that I came in fourth runner-up. Actually, the three celebrities above me were all dead guys. I beat everyone but Frank Sinatra and two Elvis Presleys.

And that guy the Lord led me to pray for, Trent Carlini? He won.

QUESTIONS *for* REFLECTION

1. What is the hardest challenge you've ever had to overcome? The biggest loss you've ever endured?

2. Did you have to face this situation alone? Were there friends to support you? How did your faith encourage you?

3. Are you recovering from a traumatic event in your own life? How are you working through these issues?

4. How can you prepare yourself to help others who are going through a crisis or loss?

Chapter Ten

GREAT MOMENTS in PRESIDENTIAL PUNKING

G ETTING "PUNKED" IS nothing new.

Long before Allen Funt and *Candid Camera* or Ashton Kutcher and MTV, people have been fooling one another for fun and profit. Even the Bible records its fair share of impersonator pranks, though few of them were for the purest of motives.

In Genesis, Rebekah and her son Jacob pulled the old switch-eroo on Jacob's twin brother, Esau, and their father, Isaac. In their Jewish tradition, the firstborn son would normally inherit the lion's share of his father's wealth, as well as the all-important blessing. Esau was just a few moments older than Jacob, but his mother wanted everything to go to Jacob. As Isaac lay blind and feeble on his deathbed, Rebekah dressed Jacob in his brother's clothes, covered his hands with goat hair, and prepared Isaac's favorite meal for her husband. Even though Isaac was suspicious and repeatedly questioned Jacob, the smell of Esau's clothes and the touch of his son's hairy hands were enough to fool him. A father's blessing was irrevocable, and Jacob succeeded in taking what belonged to his brother.

But turnabout is fair play, and years later Jacob was on the receiving end of a doozie of a prank involving another first-born child.

After Isaac's death, Jacob fled his family home because he feared payback from Esau. As he journeyed, Jacob came upon a well where his uncle's flocks were being watered. Suddenly, his eyes fell upon Rachel, one of the shepherdesses, whose beauty made him fall down on his knees and weep. Jacob immediately asked her father, his uncle Laban, for her hand in marriage. In those days, the bride's parents received a financial dowry from the groom. Apparently, Jacob had left home without his American Express card and didn't have any of his father's inheritance handy in large, unmarked bills, so Jacob promised to work for his uncle for seven years—*seven years!*—so he could marry Rachel.

Seven years came and went. The wedding was a blur of drinking and feasting and more drinking. When Jacob woke up the morning after his marriage, he looked across the bed and realized that he had actually married Rachel's older sister, Leah! Laban explained that it was his people's custom for the older daughter to be married first, but if Jacob was willing to work another seven years, Jacob could take Rachel, the younger daughter, for his bride as well. Wow! Payback can be tough.

There's something in the human heart that likes to fool other people, even if it's only for fun. When it's that kind of punking, you can count me in! Every new morning promises some new adventure. Each new city presents some new opportunity.

In 2004, I had an engagement in Boston that took me right by presidential candidate John Kerry's Democratic Convention headquarters. I just couldn't pass up something this fun, so I stopped in for a visit. The campaign was hectically preparing for its convention there at the Fleet Center, and they apparently didn't have any extra staff to watch the door. So I walked right in—like I owned the place, or rather, like I was an incumbent president who went anywhere he dang well pleased. I made my way to the center of the room, commanded everyone's attention, then in my most serious Texas accent announced, "I just came by to check out the competition!"

I must confess that punking is addictive. Wherever I go, I have the opportunity to lift the mood and hearts of the people I meet. Usually the person I've punked turns from "punkee" to "punker."

I was standing backstage at the 2006 Gospel Music Awards when I saw Grammy, Dove, Stellar, and American Music Award-winning artist Kirk Franklin. Kirk is already a very animated guy, so when I tapped him on the shoulder, he almost jumped out of his shoes. After he got over the shock, a sly grin appeared on his face. "Hey," he said, "let's go back to the dressing room where my band and singers are getting ready. Send your 'Secret Service' agents in and I'll follow, telling my guys that the president wants to meet them!" That's exactly what we did. Needless to say, the whole room was in shock, and there, over in the corner, was Kirk Franklin, laughing himself silly!

In January of 2008, I was in Atlanta for an event planners' convention when it occurred to me that the world's largest cable news network was just a few miles away. I was staying with lifelong friends Joel and Trace Balin. They have a friend from church who happened to work at Turner Broadcasting's Cable News Network. We arranged to meet at the CNN Center around noon. The Center itself is actually a fourteen-story office structure with an interior atrium that houses their network offices, as well as retail businesses and restaurants. As we entered the facility, huge JumboTron screens were carrying an important news conference with President Bush live from the Middle East. We were escorted through the security area and onto the main floor of the bustling newsroom. Immediately, every eye shifted from the TV monitors onto me...and then back to the TV monitors...and back to me again.

In their very presence was the man they were watching via satellite, wearing the same blue tie and flag lapel pin. I looked around at everyone and said, "Hey, do you think I'm dumb enough to *really go there*? It's dangerous, so I sent my look-alike!"

There were double takes.

There were triple takes.

They had been "Bush-whacked"!

Suddenly, people were grabbing their own cameras and asking for pictures with me—and then pulling me by my coat sleeve into other people's offices and cubicles to watch them get just as stupefied as they had been. It was a blast. As we made our way through the corridors of CNN, I saw screen shots of some of the most defining moments in recent American history. These people reported the news in all its glory and shame, detailing humanity's crowning achievements and unthinkable crimes. Every person I met was gracious and engaging, and I wished I had had the time to speak with them about their place in history, not only in our time, but in the eternal scheme of things.

Perhaps the most elaborate conspiracy to punk a national figure came in July of 2006 at the hands of Jerry and Jonathan Falwell, who wanted to surprise their dad, Dr. Jerry Falwell, on the occasion of their church's fiftieth anniversary celebration. Thomas Road Baptist Church was dedicating their beautiful new facility, and more than twenty thousand people were attending the outdoor festivities, which would culminate with speeches, music, and a huge fireworks display. Dr. Falwell's sons had told their father to expect a surprise guest, but neither the storied evangelist nor the enthusiastic crowd was prepared when an impressive motorcade of police motorcycles, long limousines, and even the obligatory ambulance drove—sirens wailing and lights flashing—into the Liberty University stadium. As my security detail opened the doors for me to emerge from the vehicle, Jerry's sons grew a little fearful that this would overwhelm their father, who had been in declining health for some time, so one of his boys leaned over and whispered, "Don't worry, Dad, he's just an impersonator."

I can only imagine that the Falwell family must have a fine history of practical jokes, because this seemed to make Dr. Falwell think his sons were trying to fool him into thinking that this wasn't the actual commander in chief! Jerry rose from his chair and headed straight across the stage to me. Clasping both my hands in his, he looked straight into my eyes and warmly said, "Mr. President, thank you for blessing us again with your presence here!"

What a moment! As I took my place at the podium to speak, it became increasingly obvious to everyone that I wasn't really Dubya, but it was also clear that this good-humored family prank would go down in the record books as one of the best ever.

As I shared earlier, when it comes to punking, turnabout is fair play.

I got my comeuppance on my fiftieth birthday.

Kathy knows that it's hard to prank a prankster, so she began her little conspiracy several months earlier by getting my manager to tell me that we had been invited to perform in our home town for the Florida Family Policy Council. This worthy organization, headed by my friend John Stemberger, is committed to the sanctity of human life and to the biblical model for marriage and families. I was honored to accept.

My role was to provide some comedic entertainment and then introduce the keynote speaker, a Mr. Charlson. You need to know that I am fastidious about my performances, so I always arrive early to survey the venue, do a sound check, and make sure nothing is left to chance. This drove Kathy crazy, because this event was actually a ruse for a surprise party, attended by more than 150 of our family and friends. After I was satisfied with the arrangements, I went backstage to stay out of sight until my appearance.

When "Hail to the Chief" started playing, I knew it was the cue for Kathy and me to enter the room and step onto the small stage. But as soon as I entered the doorway, I was hit with a blinding spotlight that shone directly in my eyes the whole time. I wouldn't allow myself to say anything about it; after all, the show must go on. And the audience was cheering wildly, so everything seemed to be going fine. Little did I know that only a few feet in front of me sat my parents, my sisters, and all my friends from church. Looking back, it was the kind of crowd who would gather for your funeral. The good news was that I didn't have to die to get to be there with them.

I went through my routine, played guitar, and sang, and generally hammed it up. Because I couldn't see a thing, I had no idea that Kathy was behind me making funny faces and generally mocking me when I wasn't looking.

I thought the crowd was laughing so loudly because I was so "on" that night.

Finally, the time came for me to introduce "Mr. Charlson," whose birthday happened to be that evening. As I did, Kathy corrected me by saying, "George, I think his real name is '*Charles's son*,' not *Charlson*."

When she said that, the lights went up and I saw a room packed with a lifetime full of friends and family. There in the front, along with my mom, was my father, Charles. The whole group burst into "Happy Birthday," and I doubled over in laughter with the realization that I had been presidentially punked!

Now I know how it feels to be on the receiving end of a loving prank.

And it's not so bad at all.

Author's note: Hey, I know I've stretched the impersonation metaphor further than it's probably ever been stretched, so I don't feel the necessity of having to spiritualize every single anecdote in this book. In other words, relax, kids—no Questions for Reflection homework tonight!

CHAPTER ELEVEN

MUSINGS by MOONLIGHT

You are the light of the world. A city on a hill cannot be hidden. Neither do people light a lamp and put it under a bowl. Instead they put it on its stand, and it gives light to everyone in the house. In the same way, let your light shine before men, that they may see your good deeds and praise your Father in heaven.

[MATTHEW 5:14–16]

SINCE MY WIFE punked me within an inch of my life on my fiftieth birthday, I knew Kathy would be on high alert as her fiftieth rolled around. I figured the best way to avoid being caught was to wait to the very last minute to plan it, but true to form, with great help from friends and family, everything came together just in time. There was even a measure of poetic justice: her payback party would also involve a presidential performance and a whole hoard of surprise guests.

I was scheduled to perform at an event for Orlando news-talk Radio WDBO that featured conservative pundit Neal

Boortz and Washington, D.C, political correspondent Jamie Dupree. Kathy joined me at the venue in Orlando's newly renovated Church Street Station district. After the show, one of the radio personalities who was in on the ruse asked if I could make a quick appearance at an adjacent restaurant to greet some friends and VIPs. This is a fairly common request and we are happy to oblige our hosts, so Kathy thought nothing of it.

We walked across the street and into a stylish Mexican restaurant where—per our instructions—we asked for the "Armstrong Party." We were escorted up the stairs, and when the ballroom door opened, almost one hundred of our friends and family members shouted, "Surprise!" Kathy was ushered into "The First Lady's Ball," a birthday celebration in honor of *my* first lady. The whole evening was perfect, from the flamenco dancers downstairs to "the Three Amigos" upstairs. This trio of impersonators were spot-on imitators of Steve Martin, Chevy Chase, and Martin Short. They were a riot, and included me in a re-enactment of a scene from the classic comedy film of the same name.

The Mission: Impossible team could not have pulled it off better.

After the party, I took Kathy on a surprise vacation to Cabo San Lucas, Mexico. We stayed in the beautiful home of our friend Tom Walsh, founder of the Los Cabos Children's Foundation. We have been honored to perform several times for this worthy charity, sharing the spotlight with Crystal Cathedral pastor Robert A. Schuller and entertainers Amy Grant and Vince Gill.

Tom's house is on a mountainside, and the view is nothing short of spectacular. One day, I awoke before dawn, went outside onto their extravagant deck, lit the fire pit, and lay in a thickly cushioned lounge chair to watch the coming sunrise. The moon was just a large, thin sliver hanging in the open, starlit sky. In the peace and stillness of those early hours, I listened to what God was teaching me through His creation.

The moon is an imitator of sorts. It generates no light of its own, but reflects the brilliance of its closest star, the sun. The moon appears brightest when it faces both the source of its light and the recipient of its reflection.

Similarly, my effectiveness as a professional imitator is measured by how well I reflect the attributes of George W. Bush toward my audience. I am a mirror, designed to take what is beheld and reflect it to the beholder. Likewise, my success as an imitator of God is based upon how clearly I reflect the light and life of the Father. I have no light or heat of my own; in fact, without Christ, I am just as cold and dead as the surface of the moon. In the first chapter of his Gospel, John wrote, "In him [Jesus] was life, and that life was the light of men" (v. 4), and that Christ was "the true light that gives light to every man" (v. 9).

Later in Jesus' ministry, He turned to His followers and called them to imitate His luminous nature: "You are the light of the world....Let your light shine before men, that they may see your good deeds and praise your Father in heaven (Matt. 5:14, 16).

Jesus is the sun and we are the moon.

The sun shines during the day, but the moon lights the earth in the darkness of night. Our world is in darkness, Christ is the light, and we reflect His glory so that our darkened world can know Him.

The sun/moon analogy isn't perfect, but few analogies are. The biggest difference is that believers not only reflect God's character, but can actually radiate His love, because we are in Christ and He is in us.

Do others experience the light of God's presence when we are with them? Do we demonstrate extraordinary compassion or patience? Divine kindness or otherworldly peace?

We should.

We can.

We must.

Why? Because we are God's plan to reach the world.

Paul tells the early Christians that the Lord Himself "has committed to us the ministry of reconciliation. We are therefore Christ's ambassadors, as though God were making his appeal through us" (2 Cor. 5:19–20).

You're probably thinking, "Whoa. Slow down, G-Dubya! You're saying that God wants to use hard-hearted, cynical, anxious, impatient, arrogant, despicable, two-faced, coarse, undisciplined me to change the world?"

No. God is saying it, and yes, that's His plan.

But along the way, Christ is changing you into a loving, joyful, peaceful, patient, kind, good, faithful, gentle, self-controlled likeness of Himself (Gal. 5:22–23). And the new you is what will be so appealing to the world. Your transformation will make them wonder what makes you different from how you used to be.

Listen, I know I'm not really Dubya. But I know that my lifelike impersonation of him can make people feel like they are actually in the president's presence. Chills, tears, hysteria, blubbering—I've seen the effect my imitation has upon audiences.

Shouldn't our imitation of Jesus also truly move those around us?

The sun inched over the horizon as I lay under the brightening Mexican sky that morning, pondering the mystery and majesty of God's love for us. Colors slowly appeared in the east, and I began to hear the waking sounds of the day. I started seeing the outline of the mountains that rose before the Sea of Cortez. I became aware of the stunning flowers and cacti surrounding Tom's house. The morning light illuminated the lush emerald fairways and hand-tended greens of the nearby hillside golf course. Everything was breathtaking.

I wanted to run and get my camera, to photograph the vivid colors that were sweeping across the sky and bringing the coastline into clear view, to capture the pink and purple clouds that reflected in broken patterns off the rippling waters of the sea. I pulled myself away from this dazzling panorama just long enough to grab my camera and the perfect cup of coffee.

I returned in time to see the sun creep over the mountain in a crescendo of orange light, and within seconds, I felt the warmth of its glow. I clicked photo after photo. The day was now in full swing. The sun became too bright to look at and the air too hot for comfort, but I had my photographs, my memories, and the hope of another sunrise tomorrow.

When I show friends those pictures, they ooh and aah at the images, but they are only seeing a frame of what I experienced. There is no sound, no peripheral vision, no smell of the air, or the cool of the predawn breeze. There is no way to contain the glory of that panorama in a single picture or in a thousand words. That image is but a hint of the real experience, the greater truth, the whole enchilada.

That's what we get to be: snapshots of God's glory meant to tantalize the human heart for the majesty of its Maker's love.

Be the moon, reflect the Son, and make 'em want what God has given you.

QUESTIONS *for* REFLECTION

1. Reflect on some special moments in your life when God's creation was speaking to you. What was nature telling you about its Creator?

2. Every month, the moon waxes and wanes according to its position between the sun and the earth. Using this analogy, how well do you feel you are reflecting the light of Christ? Are you a full moon? A half moon? A crescent? Or a new moon (no light)?

3. Our lives can be compelling reflections of the character of Christ. Take a few moments and ask the Lord to help you represent Him to a specific person or group of people.

4. Ask God for the strength, wisdom, and opportunity to "be the moon" in their lives in the coming days.

CHAPTER TWELVE

The FOLLY of FEARING FAILURE

"No weapon forged against you will prevail..." declares the LORD.

[ISAIAH 54:17]

I CAN'T STAND TRASH-TALK television.

When I worked at our family appliance store in Orlando, I would often make deliveries to our customers' homes. I would enter their living rooms, only to find young kids plopped down in front of the TV watching a freak show parade of sexual perversion, racism, and paternity squabbles—usually culminating in a chair-throwing, hair-pulling, profanity-laced brawl. The ratings may have been great; but the lessons were terrible, especially for children who are so prone to imitate what they see.

Still, I know human nature, how we love our voyeurism. We're tempted to feel better about ourselves by comparing our lives to the unfortunate ones on these kinds of shows. We're prone to think, "At least my life's not *that bad*," rather than, "I know this must break God's heart."

What can we do when the world we live in seems at odds with the God we serve?

I recently read a book called *Roaring Lambs*, authored by the late Emmy Award-winning television producer Bob Briner. The book challenges Christians to positively affect their culture by being a part of the culture, by letting our light shine gracefully in the marketplace. Briner's words were actually a tremendous encouragement to me as I wrote this book. I had worried that writing about my faith so openly would hurt my career. I wrestled with the fear that people would not buy my books or hire me for their events. I confess that I was concerned about the bottom line. I almost put my light under a "Bush-el," if you'll pardon the pun.

Finally, I realized that if Christians don't offer a compassionate and compelling alternative to the darkness of the world, then who will? I understood that any public platform I had been given wasn't to persuade people to love John Morgan, but rather so that they might know the love of Christ. If I respected and served my audiences, I would earn their respect. I resolved that my witness—whether spoken, written, or simply lived—would be consistent and clear. The real bottom line is serving folks with true love and excellence on behalf of Jesus and when, and only when, appropriate, sharing in a comfortable, natural way.

However, fear stands in the way of our best intentions. You've heard the expression, "You are what you eat." I disagree. I believe we are what we think. Each thought builds our faith or builds our fears.

When I was growing up, my mind was a river running with fear, and each fearful thought exposed an even deeper fear.

My fear of being ridiculed revealed my fear of rejection.

My inability to trust revealed my fear of exposure.

My fear of being beat up revealed my fear of pain.

Fears are like little terrorists. They infiltrate our brain to destroy the truth and then dictate their twisted version of reality. They try to tell us what we should do, what we can't do, and why.

Fear says, "Oh, if you ask that girl out, she'll only laugh in your face. And if you get vulnerable, you'll be found out to be the despicable excuse for a human being that you really are. Just stick with me," fear says as he throws his arm around your shoulder, "and we'll be just fine."

I was in the drama club in high school. I loved acting and the legitimate pretense it offered me to be someone else. My fellow thespians were my best friends, and the club was a bright spot during my dark teen years. Still, I only tried out for bit parts because I never believed that I was capable of more. My fearful thoughts had convinced me to play it safe.

I remember it like it was yesterday: my senior year, 1974, during the class play auditions for George Orwell's *1984*.

I had scanned the script and found an appropriately insignificant role. Surely, there would be no competition for that part. I would be safe. Then Mrs. Brown, our director, surprised the cast and crew with this announcement: "Rather than holding auditions for the lead part this year, I am awarding it to someone deserving."

I thought, "OK, it's going to Tom Pache. He's the star."

What happened next was unimaginable. "It's John Morgan!" she declared, and the whole room erupted in applause. I went flush.

It was a gift.

It was an affirmation.

It was too much. The very next day, I made up some lame excuse and quit the drama club.

For years, I believed lies about myself. I imposed sanctions on my possibilities. I caged my creativity. Looking back, I now realize that the fears didn't actually imprison me. Rather, it was my acceptance of them that did.

In truth, I wasn't fearful enough!

King David told his children, "Fear the LORD, you his saints, for those who fear him lack nothing. The lions may grow weak and hungry, but those who seek the LORD lack no good thing. Come, my children, listen to me; I will teach you the fear of the LORD (Ps. 34:9–11). In turn, Solomon, David's son, clearly proclaimed, "The fear of the LORD is the beginning of knowledge" (Prov. 1:7). Jesus himself told His followers that their fear of man was misplaced: "Do not be afraid of those who kill the body but cannot kill the soul. Rather, be afraid of the One who can destroy both soul and body in hell" (Matt. 10:28).

Sufficiency. Blessing. Wisdom. Knowledge. Eternal life. These are the products of our righteous fear of God, but they are only available to those who fear Him. Fear God and live.

When David faced Goliath, he didn't focus on the power of his opponent. Instead, he trusted in the omnipotence of his God. He understood that his Lord created the universe with a word, animated Adam with a breath, and wrote His commandments upon Moses' tablets with a finger. David's God led His nation with a pillar of flame, crushed Pharaoh's army with the weight of the sea, and made the sun stand still in the sky so that His armies could destroy their enemies.

When we focus on our own fears, we are blind to the fearsomeness of our God. We ignore His ferocious love and His unrelenting compassion. We obscure His glorious perfection and utter holiness.

We trade the confidence of His incomparable strength for the inadequacy of our own weakness. No wonder we fear! No wonder the enemy of our souls wants us think things like, "Oh, I could never fear God. He's too loving." But the spiritual reality is that we can never really love God without truly fearing Him.

Only the fear of something greater can destroy a lesser fear.

Only the love for something greater can replace a lesser love.

Fearing failure can be replaced by the worship of a fearsome God who is our champion, strong tower, and mighty fortress.

I was transformed by this truth as I listened to a sermon at an outdoor Christian festival. The speaker challenged us to surrender every part of our lives to Christ. Until that point, I had believed another lie. I had rationalized that it was impossible to totally surrender our lives to Christ, because that would make us perfect; and since no one attains perfection in this life, then God couldn't possibly demand that level of obedience from any of us. Because it wouldn't be fair for God to ask this of us, that meant that we were excused to live lives characterized by the occasional sin or two.

Sounds good, doesn't it?

Most lies do. Why else would we want to believe them?

The Holy Spirit used this speaker to expose that lie. God challenged me to yield 100 percent of my life to Christ in that very moment. I didn't have to worry about the next week or the next day or the next hour. I decided that His total lordship of my life would start with that moment.

Suddenly, I knew God was right and I was wrong. I stood at the end of that sermon, along with dozens of others, yielding my life fully to the control of God. I was so scared that my legs were literally shaking. This was new terrain for me. What would happen next? I went up after the service and shared my fear with the minister who had so effectively led me into this new paradigm. "I was shaking like a leaf," I told him as I described my decision to accept his challenge. A sympathetic smile broke across his face as he said, "That's because you don't really know Him yet." He added, "No one is more loving, kind, and trustworthy than Jesus. Trust me, son, you won't be disappointed."

And he was right.

Over the years, I've learned that Jesus only asks me to do what is the very best thing for me to do. Everything else is a lie—and every day is a quest to remember this.

As I've grown spiritually, there are new lies to fight and new levels of faith to attain. Satan is relentless with his onslaught. But God is even more relentless with His grace.

What if I fail?

What if they ridicule me?

What if they kill me?

It really doesn't matter, because being obedient to God is everything. When we listen to our fears and question God's loving direction, we exclude ourselves from the very adventure into which we've been called.

What excuse is standing between your fear and God's blessing? What doubt is silencing your voice to a world that needs to hear about Jesus? What lies are keeping you in a prison of your own device? As the apostle Paul wrote, "It is for freedom that Christ has set us free. Stand firm, then, and do not let yourselves be burdened again by a yoke of slavery" (Gal. 5:1).

So I now challenge you as I once was challenged.

Will you take a leap of faith and in this moment yield 100 percent of your life to God?

Will you open every closet door and allow Christ to transform everything inside?

Will you replace the fear of failure with the fear of the Almighty?

Will you allow God to use you to touch your world for His glory?

Because if and when you do, you've taken your next step into a life of adventure with God where "'no weapon forged against you will prevail, and you will refute every tongue that accuses you. This is the heritage of the servants of the LORD, and this is their vindication from me,' declares the LORD" (Isa. 54:17).

QUESTIONS *for* REFLECTION

1. Fear is a real spiritual force that attacks every human being. We fear rejection, exposure, and failure, not to mention sickness and death. How have these fears affected your life?

2. What, if anything, has broken the cycle of fear in your own life?

3. How can the acceptance, love, and presence of Christ dethrone and destroy the effect of fear in our lives?

4. How can you graciously share this good news with a fearful, anxious world?

CHAPTER THIRTEEN

STORIES FROM the ROAD

The steps of a good man are ordered by the LORD: and he delighteth in his way.

[PSALM 37:23, KJV]

AUGUST 2004: SKYDIVING

Kathy loves heights. I do too, but she does more. So the summer George H. W. Bush turned eighty and went skydiving for his birthday, Kathy decided to treat me to skydiving for mine. "Oh boy," I said, only half-heartedly.

We were performing in Las Vegas that weekend, so we drove out into the Nevada desert and met these two terrorists—uh, I mean, fun-loving skydiving instructors. They gave us a quick tutorial and stuck us in a stripped-out plane. We had to sign a bunch of releases, agreeing not to sue and basically giving them our house and kids if anything happened to us.

You know, you never think the unthinkable is going to happen to you, but my parachute didn't open right. We jumped tandem style, which means if the chute doesn't open, you get to break your trainer's fall.

The instructor and I were dropping like a rock, but I didn't know it. I was blissfully unaware of how close I was to Jesus. Just before the emergency chute deployed, the main chute became untangled, and we landed safely. Kathy's flight was without incident, except that she got a little queasy. Her terrorist—I mean instructor—told her to just use her shirt if she got sick. Kathy said she considered vomiting on *his shirt* just for saying that.

January 2006: Audacity

We were in New York City for a gig. I'd wanted to get on Barbara Walter's ABC show, *The View*, ever since I punked her at the Bush inaugural, so we found out where they were shooting and went over to the studios. There was a huge line of people outside the building, waiting to get tickets for the show. I walked right past the line of people, entered the closed door, went up to the girl behind the counter, and in my best Bush voice said, "I want to get on *The View*." She smiled and exclaimed, "Oh my goodness, it's the president!" After taking pictures with her and her coworkers, she said, "Well, Mr. President, it just doesn't work that way." I joked, "How about you calling upstairs to your producers, and tell 'em to come down and see me." She did and they did—and sure enough, they gave me a small role in the show that day.

When I'm in character as the president, I have a boldness that I wouldn't ordinarily have. This confidence has helped me land serendipitous appearances twice on *The View*, as well as on *The Today Show*, *Good Morning America*, *The Tony*

Danza Show, Fox News *DaySide*, Channel 7 in Chicago, and a host of other radio and television shows.

It's fun to walk in another man's shoes, especially if that man is someone we admire and want to emulate. As imitators of Jesus, we are actually entrusted with the power and authority He's given us. That is why Jesus instructed His followers to heal the sick, cast out demons, and preach the gospel to the poor in His name. When we act humbly but confidently on His behalf, our audacity comes from His authority, and that's what moves mountains.

APRIL 2006: THE GUITAR PULL

I have always been a big fan of world-class guitarist singer/songwriter Phil Keaggy. Every year during Gospel Music Week in Nashville, our PR company hosts a guitar pull for musicians and media. Even though I'm not a musical recording artist per se, I was invited to make a surprise appearance and perform a song. For me, the kicker was that Phil Keaggy would also be in the room. In the weeks prior to the event, I practiced endlessly, so that I wouldn't embarrass myself. Musical comedian Justin Fennell helped me write a patriotic parody version of James Taylor's "Steamroller Blues," which we appropriately retitled, "The Red, White, and Blues."

I'm no virtuoso, but when my turn came around, I held my own. During the musical interlude, I said, "Take it, Phil," and my guitar hero played a rousing blues solo over my three-chord vamp. I exclaimed, "I can't believe I'm jammin' with Phil Keaggy!" to which he exclaimed, "I can't believe I'm jammin' with the president!" I could have gone home happy right then and there, but the conference lasted several more days.

Matt McPherson, the renowned guitar maker, was also at the showcase. Most of the musicians in the room were using his magnificent instruments. The next day, I was chatting in the hotel suite with Matt and mentioned that I was scheduled to perform the following night at the Dove Awards. I blurted out, "You know, Matt, it sure would look good for G. W. to be playing a Mac," then quickly apologized for being so manipulative. Matt replied, "Well, John, you're right; you were—but it's also a great idea." He offered to loan me his personal guitar. I was overjoyed! The next night I played it onstage at the Grand Old Opry. In the middle of my performance, I looked down and quipped, "A McPherson guitar; very presidential." The Nashville crowd cheered.

As I exited the stage, my cell phone rang. It was Matt, "Good job, John! Why don't you just take that guitar home with you?"

What a thrill!

January–March 2007: Winter Jam

As a young believer in the 1980s, I thought I was God's gift to Christian music. It took decades for me to understand that humility and love, not pride and pretense, are what please God. To my surprise, after He had purified my flawed ambition, the Lord placed me on Christian music's biggest annual concert tour, Winter Jam. That year's lineup included multi-platinum artists Steven Curtis Chapman and Jeremy Camp, and featured up-and-comers Sanctus Real, Hawk Nelson, and Britt Nicole. The tour crisscrossed America in six busses and three semi trailers, playing before an average of eight thousand people each night in more than thirty cities.

My son Stephen traveled with me as my road manager, helping me with my merchandise and also setting up the battery-powered car that our sponsor, ZAP Automotive, provided as a grand prize for a promotional drawing.

After every show, we would pack everything back into the trucks and then crawl into the crypt-like bunks that were stacked three high and two wide on each side of the bus. The first experience in my claustrophobic cocoon was disorienting, to say the least. My bladder placed a middle of the night wake-up call to my brain, which had totally forgotten that I was in the top bunk of a rolling hotel. After falling from my berth into the darkened—and locked—sleeping lounge, I had no idea how to open the door that led to the restroom. I couldn't see any doorknobs or handles by the soft glow of the green LED night lights. As my bladder grew more and more insistent, I grew more and more panicky, but alas, there was nothing I could do but shimmy back up into my bunk until someone rescued me from my locked corridor. Several hours—and many prayers—later, the tour chaplain told me the secret. He said this was a deluxe coach and everything was remote controlled. To open the doors, all I had to do was press those green LED's!

Each night my performance slot was right between Steven Curtis Chapman and Jeremy Camp. I usually did a solo guitar "thing" as part of my set, but on the last night of the tour, Jeremy's full band surprised me by playing for me, and Stephen Curtis jumped in and jammed as well. God has an amazing way of giving us the desires that He has put in our hearts.

Summer 2007: Freedom Alliance Tour

The Freedom Alliance raises funds to provide scholarships to children of our military who are killed or wounded. In 2007, conservative talk-show host Sean Hannity and Col. Oliver North hosted a five-city Freedom Concert arena tour to benefit this patriotic cause. I was honored to be invited to participate with Teresa Barnwell, America's leading Hillary Clinton impersonator. Teresa and I had been performing a show called *The Great Debate*, a comedic sparring match about leadership. We were to present an abridged version for the tour.

Basically, Dubya would be announced as a surprise guest, enter to the music, and the audience would cheer it up good. I would eventually get around to raggin' on Hillary. Teresa would sneak up behind me, tap me on the shoulder, and comedic sparks would fly, to the delight of the audience. At the end of each performance, we would set aside our partisan politics in support of the children of America's soldiers. It was a hoot and afforded us the opportunity to meet a whole host of Republican heavyweights. We met presidential hopefuls Mayor Rudy Giuliani, Governor Mitt Romney, and Senator Fred Thompson. We also met House Speaker Newt Gingrich, Texas governor Rick Perry, and Senator Kay Bailey Hutchison. World-class entertainment was provided by music legends Lee Greenwood, Charlie Daniels, LeAnn Rimes, Collin Raye, Montgomery Gentry, Michael W. Smith, and comedian Larry the Cable Guy.

The greatest moment of each evening came when some military family members in attendance were surprised by a live video feed from their loved ones serving in harm's way overseas. They were the real stars of the show, and to them we owe untold gratitude and honor.

QUESTIONS *for* REFLECTION

1. Although most Americans believe in God, according to an October 2006 Harris poll, less than one-third of them believe that He is actively involved in the details of our lives. What do you think?

2. Do you think that God enjoys blessing His children and laughs when they are happy?

3. Have you ever held dreams or aspirations that were never realized the way you thought they might be, but were somehow fulfilled in a better time or place? If so, what were they?

4. What dreams and plans are you willing to place in the Lord's hands, believing that He will guide you on your life's journey?

CHAPTER 14

LOVING the FIRST LADY FIRST

For this reason a man will leave his father and mother and be united to his wife, and the two will become one flesh." This is a profound mystery—but I am talking about Christ and the church.

[EPHESIANS 5:31–32]

Behind every great man, there is a great woman rolling her eyes.

I know that's the case in the Morgan household, and I'll even bet it's true every so often at the Bush homestead.

Think about it; just a few month's after George W. Bush and Laura Lane Welch got home from their honeymoon, he hit the campaign trail pursuing what would be an unsuccessful bid for the US House of Representatives.

I can imagine Laura's response: *Geo-orge!*

Then a decade and twin daughters later, Dubya put together a group of investors to purchase the Texas Rangers baseball team.

Owning a baseball team! Wow! That's every red-blooded

American man's dream—and most red-blooded American woman's!

Five years later, George was a long shot to unseat popular incumbent Democratic Texas governor Ann Richards.

You want to run for what?

Bush won that election by five percentage points but then was re-elected for a second term by a landslide. Within a year, he decided to make a run for president of the United States—and triumphed!

At some point along the way, I'll bet the eyes didn't roll quite as much. In fact, George attributes much of his success to Laura, who challenged him to stop drinking and get serious about his faith and future.

They make it so easy for Kathy and I to imitate them. In our hearts, they are not just "the first couple," but George and Laura Bush are the epitome of a great marriage, truly worthy of our imitation.

There is no doubt that he respects her intelligence and grace and that she respects his passion and integrity. It is rare to see a couple who look up to one another as they do. In public, they stare proudly at each other like they are one another's biggest fans, because they are. And in private, it is no secret that they pray and worship together.

Kathy is truly my first lady.

As I've said, I spent my teenage years living in a godless, loveless vacuum, until, at the age of eighteen, I gave my life back to my Creator. This decision truly changed everything. Yet, I was burdened by so much baggage from my past, by many skeletons in my closet, by many issues I was still dealing with. I believed the lie that I had disqualified myself from true love.

One Sunday, my pastor was teaching on the subject of faith. At the conclusion of his sermon, he instructed everyone who wanted to trust God for something miraculous to stand. I immediately thought, "Wow! How about a wife? That would be amazing!" So I stood, along with others who had their own requests, and asked God to give me a wife. I even wrote my simple prayer on the inside back cover of my Bible: "Lord, I pray for a wife, according to Your will and for Your glory. Amen."

That weekend, at a church retreat, Kathy and I met at the beach. But we didn't *just meet*. For both of us, it was one of those intensely romantic moments you see in the movies.

My heart exploded within me when I saw her.

I was blown away. And so was she.

That was Memorial Day weekend. Three months later, I planned an elaborate retreat for Labor Day weekend back at the beach with all the friends who were there when we first met. No one but our Bible study leader knew that I had chosen that time and place to ask Kathy to be my wife. We peeled away from the crowd for a romantic dinner together. After our meal, we lingered over our tiramisu dessert until I couldn't wait a moment longer. My heart was pounding and my endorphins were swimming. I was paying so much attention to Kathy that she mistook my intensity for enthusiasm about her discourse on scented drawer liners. Unable to get a word in edgewise, I finally had to interrupt our small talk with, "Will you marry me?"

At this point, she had caught her breath, dismissed what she was sure I hadn't said, and launched back into her topic.

I interrupted again, "Because if you will, I have something for you," and slipped her engagement ring box from its hiding place in my sock and placed it before her on the linen table-cloth. She paused, re-connected with reality, and then squeaked out an emphatic, "Yes!" We hugged, and I felt God smile. We headed back to the beach to celebrate with all our friends. Later, I capped off that unforgettable evening by standing underneath her window with my guitar and serenading her.

We were married on Valentine's Day weekend in 1982, and a year and nine months later, our first son was born on Thanksgiving Day. Kathy and I like to say we have a "holiday marriage."

Our first years together were wonderful but challenging. As a child, Kathy's family life was marked by divorce and brokenness. She suffered from a fear of abandonment that I hadn't experienced and built a protective wall that kept her from fully trusting me. I didn't know what to do. One night, after a dinner conversation with our good friends Pastor Mike and Cindy Gilland, we began to work through what we couldn't see on our own.

We all have blind spots in our lives, and the loving counsel of our pastoral team has continued to help us grow together. Kathy and I owe the success of our marriage to the grace of God, expressed through the relationships we enjoy at our church. We cannot overstate the importance of being a part of a great local fellowship. Kathy and I are grateful members of Metro Life Church in Orlando. They have tremendous marriage resources and are blessed with a wonderful track record of successful and restored marriages.

The fifth chapter of Ephesians begins with Paul's call for us to be imitators of God and ends with Paul's insistence that husbands and wives respect and love one another deeply. If we are to be true imitators of Christ, we must reflect His love in the way we love our spouses. Woven into verses 22 through

33 are the hallmarks of that love: mutual submission, mutual sacrifice, and mutual care.

But Paul takes the analogy even farther. Not only does the way we love our spouse indicate how well we imitate Jesus, but the way a husband and wife care for one another should truly reflect the love that Christ and the church have for one another.

> "For this reason a man will leave his father and mother and be united to his wife, and the two will become one flesh." This is a profound mystery—but I am talking about Christ and the church. However, each one of you also must love his wife as he loves himself, and the wife must respect her husband.
> —Ephesians 5:31–33

This is an honor beyond words.

Not only are we entrusted with the privilege of being God's loving imitators, but husbands and wives are called to be living pictures of the love that Jesus, the Groom, has for His Bride, the church. God's Word clearly describes marriage as the "one flesh" union of one man and one women, because marriage is symbolic of the Lamb's Wedding Feast in heaven.

My responsibility is to love Kathy as Christ loved the church and laid down His life for her. Her responsibility is to love and respect me as the church does Christ. That leaves no room for abuse, cruelty, mistreatment, or neglect—only love.

When Kathy tagged me to impersonate Dubya, she had no idea that I would pull her in as Laura. Neither did I.

So how did the whole Laura Bush thing come about?

It began when I started getting some requests to appear as

a couple. (I'm good, but I'm not *that* good!) Our first thought was to ask one of our best friends, Bonnie Anderson, who naturally looks more like Laura than Kathy, but then I started daydreaming how much fun it would be to perform with my wife and wondered if Kathy would even consider the idea.

It wasn't a big leap of faith. We bought a wig, Kathy tried it on—and out popped Laura! What a surprise.

One of our first "first couple" gigs was an appearance at a Christmas party at the home of some ardent Republicans in Los Angeles. We got directions to the upscale neighborhood and were told there would be a lot of cars—especially a big Hummer—out in front of a highly decorated home.

We got out of our rental car, walked boldly up the steps, and rang the doorbell.

The folks who answered said, "Oh look, George and Laura Bush have come to our Christmas party," and let us in. Kathy and I did our best routine, but it didn't really seem to connect. People were pleasant, but not really "getting it." About twenty minutes went by until the party's host finally came up to us and said, "OK, we give in! Who put you up to this?" Kathy and I gave each other a puzzled look and responded, "We thought *you* did!"

Awkward…

It turned out that the White House-themed Christmas party was actually a block over and that we had stumbled into a different party with a Hummer out front. The host went on to inform us that her home was the only Democratic enclave for miles and that her Republican neighbors on the next block were probably wondering where we were.

When we got to the right White House, we entertained to the sounds of "Hail to the Chief" and were greeted by a fervent, enthusiastic group of new friends. It turned out to be a wonderful night after all.

Now Kathy and I travel together, and whether she plays Laura or not, she is not usually far from my side. Our friends tell us that she often gives me that "I'm your biggest fan" look, and I give as good as I get.

And by the way, Kathy still stands behind me and rolls her eyes from time to time.

QUESTIONS *for* REFLECTION

1. What role models influenced the way you think and feel about marriage? Are they largely positive or negative?

2. How does Paul's teaching on marriage in Ephesians 5 conflict or concur with your thoughts?

3. God wants us to trust His guidance in our most intimate relationships. In which relationships do you sense the greatest need for His leadership and presence?

4. Consider giving the Lord permission to help you reflect Christ's self-sacrificial love in your most personal relationships.

CHAPTER 15

BEHIND the SCENES of the GREATEST SHOW on EARTH

*And we know that in all things God works for the good
of those who love him, who have been called according
to his purpose. For those God foreknew he also predestined to be conformed to the likeness of his Son, that
he might be the firstborn among many brothers.*

[ROMANS 8:28–29]

EVERY ONCE IN a while, someone will ask Kathy and
me, "Did you know that you looked like George and Laura
Bush when you got married?" It's a funny question, consid-
ering that we got hitched twenty years before Dubya ran for
president.

Although we didn't know, God knew.

Who else could have given me this face? And my undiscov-
ered talent for comedy?

What other power could have put me in just the right place
at just the right time to meet just the right people?

How can you explain the endless coincidences, the amazing

providences, the happy accidents?

But more than that, what can account for the change of heart that transformed me from loser to leader?

A story like mine is so unlikely, it would have a hard time passing for fiction, much less as fact. And yet, *My Life as a Bush* is true.

Far more miraculous is the reality that the Author of my story is also writing millions of other stories just as unique and satisfying. Imagine millions and millions of individual stories interacting and intertwining for one united purpose: God's glory and our good.

This is the good news of the gospel and the central theme of human history. He created us to know Him. Sin, however, blocks our fellowship with God. "For all have sinned and fall short of the glory of God" (Rom. 3:23).

God promised that He would provide the remedy. Predicted and recorded in literally hundreds of scriptural prophecies, God stepped onto the soil of Earth as Jesus, who was fully God and fully man. He became our ransom, freeing us from the prison of our sin, and opening the way for each man and woman, boy and girl, to be reconciled back to God. Jesus did this by taking our sins upon Himself and suffering our punishment on the cross. This is the greatness of God's love for us and the best news in all the world.

God has opened the way for us to know Him and have a personal relationship with Him. We were born for this. If you haven't yet experienced this, you can!

You can be reconciled to God by repenting of your sins, asking for God's forgiveness, accepting Jesus' sacrifice on the cross on your behalf, and turning your life over to Him.

Romans 3:23–24 says, "For all have sinned and fall short of the glory of God, and are justified freely by his grace, through the redemption that came by Christ Jesus."

Blows your mind, doesn't it? God-stuff usually does. After all, "In all things God works for the good of those who love Him" (Rom. 8:28).

That is the behind-the-scenes secret that the apostle Paul reveals to the early Christians in Rome who are facing persecution and execution for their beliefs. That is the life-changing power that allows us to live confidently by faith, free from the fear of failure or regret.

There is an exercise that corporate trainers often do to help leaders discover their true calling in life. They ask, "What would you try to achieve if time and money were no object and if you knew that you couldn't fail?" Oddly enough, contemporary business leaders are often better at asking this question than contemporary church leaders. This seems ironic because people living "in the world" don't have unlimited time, money, or resources. But we who are in Christ serve a God for whom "a day is like a thousand years" (2 Pet. 3:8) and who owns "the cattle on a thousand hills" (Ps. 50:10).

Every believer is called to live in the courage and confidence that God is sovereign over every detail of their lives.

In contrast, an October 2006 Harris poll reported that less than 30 percent of Americans believe that God actually controls events on Earth. When Paul says that God works *all things* for His glory and our good, what things are excluded?

That's right: no things! Because God uses *all* things!

The Lord wants us to pursue His calling with reckless abandon. We do not need to fear the untried or unknown because God is orchestrating every detail and redeeming every outcome.

How does your heart feel about this good news? Why don't you ask it?

They say that for every silver lining, there's a cloud. Here's the bad news: did you know that there is a spiritual force committed to your failure? The Bible calls him Satan, Lucifer, or the devil. He is real, and Scriptures tell us that he is a thief, a murderer, and a liar (John 10:9). If Satan cannot keep you from the knowledge of salvation, then he will try to distort the truth about your new status in Christ. He will feed you lies about who Jesus is and who you are, so that you will not trust His love for you. If the devil can't steal your soul, he'll try to steal your joy and keep you from being a joy-filled imitator of God's Son.

As a young man, I allowed Satan to blind me to the truth and power of the good news. Then, when I became a new creation in Christ, I swallowed the devil's lie that I wasn't good enough to be forgiven, much less to enjoy God's blessings. However, the deep love of God, discovered through time spent in His Word, quieted those echoing fears in my heart and replaced them with His own comforting presence.

We read in Romans 8 that God knew the end of the story before He penned the first word, that He foreknew and predestined me to be just like His Son, whom He would send as a ransom for my sin and the sin of the whole world. You and I are part of that world that "God so loved" in John 3:16.

You and I are also experiencing God's intertwining purpose this very moment as you read these words. I have the privilege of looking across this page to you and telling you that the Lord took a messed-up, self-centered, sin-addicted imposter and poured His love and life into me.

As He poured Himself in, I couldn't help but pour out the old, dead, rotting self that used to be me, a process that continues. I am learning to love others as I once only loved myself.

As He poured Himself into me, I began to take on some of His traits—love, peace, patience, kindness—attributes that I never had on my own.

As His Spirit opened the eyes of my heart, I began to see that the world is not just brick and mortar, wood and steel, earth and sky. Rather, it's a battlefield for the hearts and souls of wounded and dying people that God created to bear His image and to share His fellowship. I am learning to ache with those who hurt, weep with those who mourn, and to be an agent of His reconciliation.

I have been privileged to stand backstage in theaters, television tapings, and arenas. Without a doubt, what goes on behind the scenes is far more intentional and detailed than what is evident to the audience. There is endless scripting, rehearsal, costuming, lighting, and set design. The producer and director oversee every aspect of the show to ensure that it is creative and compelling.

Similarly, the Lord has blessed me with the honor of playing a part in His grand drama. To those who would join me on His stage, I assure you that God is the writer, director, and producer of the greatest show on Earth and has awarded you an exhilarating role on behalf of Jesus, His Son.

I have caught a glimpse behind the curtain and can tell you that this is not the day to quit the drama club, to miss out on the grand adventure.

Today is the day to say yes.

Each moment is another opportunity to experience deeper levels of trust and higher realms of faith, to become an imitator of God.

QUESTIONS *for* REFLECTION

1. What have been the two or three greatest insights you have received from your reading of this book?

2. How has the call to intentionally imagine the indwelling person of Jesus transformed your attitudes?

3. Have you identified the specific fears and self-doubts that are keeping you from God's great adventure and asked the Lord to eradicate them and replace them with confidence and joy?

4. Is there a particular person or group of people to whom God seems to be calling you to share this message of hope and reconciliation?

EPILOGUE

THE PRIVILEGE OF impersonating the commander in chief means nothing in comparison with the honor of imitating the Savior. No matter what temporary benefit I have enjoyed by resembling George W. Bush, it pales when compared to the joy of imaging Jesus Christ, God's Son, who makes His home in me. While representing Dubya is an earthly career, becoming like Jesus is an eternal calling. Not only for me, but for all of us who have accepted His invitation to eternal life.

I've had it easy. Many New Testament believers were jailed, beaten, stoned to death, sawed in half, crucified, fed to wild beasts, boiled in oil, or beheaded because of their resemblance to Jesus. Over the past two millennia, Christians have been the victims of social discrimination, economic persecution, and religious genocide. In fact, more martyrs have given their lives for Christ over the past one hundred years than in the previous nineteen centuries combined.

Why would so many people give so much to be like Jesus?

The answer is that the very best the world can offer cannot begin to compare to the riches of grace that will be ours in knowing Christ for eternity, and no trial we endure on Earth will compare to the joy that will be ours in heaven. As the apostle Paul wrote:

But what things were gain to me, these I have counted loss for Christ. Yet indeed I also count all things loss for the excellence of the knowledge of Christ Jesus my Lord, for whom I have suffered the loss of all things, and count them as rubbish, that I may gain Christ.
—Philippians 3:7–8

People frequently ask me what my plan is after President George W. Bush leaves office. I'm inclined to say, "Just look for me to keep on imitating."

And that will be 100 percent accurate.

For More Information or to Contact the Author

www.georgebushimpersonator.com